THE BRADSHAW GARDENING GUIDES

Get up to date on the most important developments in gardening technology — the newest machines, chemicals, seeds, gardening aids and methods — and profit from John Bradshaw's many years of experience at the same time. This all-new series is the definitive guide to the what, why, where and how of successful modern gardening in 16 fully illustrated volumes.

- The Lawn Book
- Growing Gourmet Vegetables
- Annual Flowers
- The Indoor Plant Primer
- The Complete Book of Bulbs
- Evergreens
- Perennial Flowers
- A Guide to the Balcony Garden
- The Shrubbery Book
- Growing Garden Fruit
- Roses
- A Guide to Children's Gardens
- Biennials for the Specialty Garden
- The Book of Trees
- The Landscaping Manual
- Controlling Garden Pests

John Bradshaw

The Indoor Plant Primer

Selection, Care and Landscaping

McClelland and Stewart

McClelland and Stewart Limited
The Canadian Publishers
25 Hollinger Road
Toronto, Ontario
M4B 3G2

CANADIAN CATALOGUING IN PUBLICATION DATA

Bradshaw, John, 1916-
   The indoor plant primer

(Bradshaw gardening guides ; 4)
Includes index.
ISBN 0-7710-1552-6
1. Indoor gardening. I. Title. II. Series:
Bradshaw, John, 1916 - Bradshaw gardening guides ; 4.

SB419.B72   635.9'65   C82-094834-9

Design and Illustrations: Pamela Patrick/Anodos Studios
Design Concept: R.K. Studios
Photography: Pamela Patrick and Susan Sheppard Irvine

Special thanks to Kensington Flower Market and The Plant
Warehouse, Toronto.
Cover: Indoor greenhouse and spa designed and built by Michael and
Peter Irvine, Toronto.

Printed and Bound in United States of America.

About The Author

Born in the famed Garden Belt of the Niagara Peninsula, John Bradshaw is today one of horticulture's best-known writers and broadcasters, as well as being one of the most widely travelled. His information is gathered first-hand from the major garden areas of the world. Every year he visits the bulb fields of Holland, the flower fields of California, the All-America Trial Grounds, the major meetings of the American and Canadian Nurserymen's Associations and the American Horticultural Council. His simple down-to-earth style of writing has introduced many beginners to the relaxing pleasure of gardening and television and radio audiences know him well.

Contents

INTRODUCTION 9
  Light 10
  Temperature 10
  Humidity 11
  Watering 12
  Feeding 15
  Care of Leaves 15
  Air 17
  Soil Mixtures 17
  Indoor Plant Hospital 18
  Increasing Your Stock from Seed 18
  Taking Cuttings 19
  Air-Layering 20
  Insect Pests and Diseases 21

AFRICAN VIOLETS 23
ASPIDISTRAS 26
CACTI 28
CALADIUM 31
CAPE PRIMROSES 34
CARNIVOROUS PLANTS 36
CHINESE EVERGREENS 38
CISSUS 40
CITRUS TREES 41

COLEUS	44
CORDYLINES	46
CROTONS	48
DIEFFENBACHIAS	50
DRACAENAS	52
FLOWERING CACTI	53
FERNS	56
FICUS	59
GARDENIAS	63
GLOXINIAS	65
HOYAS	68
IMPATIENS	71
NARCISSUS	72
NORFOLK ISLAND PINE	74
PALMS	76
PHILODENDRONS	79
PONYTAIL PALM	81
POTHOS	82
REX BEGONIAS	84
STRAWBERRY BEGONIAS	88
SCHEFFLERAS	90
SPIDER PLANTS	91
SUCCULENTS	93
INDEX	96

QUICK REFERENCE FOR LIGHT, MOISTURE & WARMTH NEEDS

SHADY AND COOL	NORTH	ASPIDISTRA, FERNS, FICUS PUMILA & IVY, MARANTA, FATSIA, FALSE ARALIA O.K. IF GIVEN BETTER LIGHT SOMETIMES: PHILODENDRON, SCHEFFLERA, DRACAENA, CHINESE EVERGREEN
LIGHT, BUT SUNLESS	NORTH	AFRICAN VIOLET, CAPE PRIMROSE, CALADIUM, CHINESE EVERGREEN, CISSUS, CORDYLINE, CROTON, DRACAENA, DIEFFENBACHIA, FLOWERING CACTI, FICUS, PHILODENDRON, SPIDER PLANT, POTHOS & FUSCHIA, MONSTERA, WANDERING JEW
SOME DIRECT SUNLIGHT, OR GOOD ARTIFICIAL LIGHT	SOUTH	FLOWERING HOUSE PLANTS, HOYA, DIEFFENBACHIA, NORFOLK ISLAND PINE, PALMS, PONYTAIL PALM, REX BEGONIA, STRAWBERRY BEGONIA, SCHEFFLERA
SUNNY WINDOW	SOUTH	CACTI AND SUCCULENTS, CITRUS, COLEUS, IMPATIENS, NARCISSUS & GERANIUM, PASSION FLOWER, KALANCHOE, HIBISCUS, EUPHORBIA, BOUGAINVILLEA
ABLE TO WITHSTAND DRY ATMOSPHERE		CACTI & SUCCULENTS, PONYTAIL PALM, SPIDER PLANT & SANSEVIERA, WANDERING JEW, PILEA * KEEP MOIST BUT DON'T SPRAY: MAIDENHAIR FERN, REX BEGONIA
NEED MOIST ATMOSPHERE – SYRINGE REGULARLY		FICUS, DIEFFENBACHIA, CISSUS, CITRUS, CHINESE EVERGREEN, COLEUS, CORDYLINE, CROTON, FLOWERING CACTI, FERNS* HOYA, GARDENIA, GLOXINIA, IMPATIENS, PALMS, PHILODENDRON, POTHOS, STRAWBERRY BEGONIA, SCHEFFLERA.
ABLE TO WITHSTAND COLD (40°F)		ASPIDISTRA, CISSUS, SPIDER PLANT, PHILODENDRON, STRAWBERRY BEGONIA, DRACAENA
ABLE TO WITHSTAND GAS FUMES & SMOKE		BEST ARE THICK-LEAVED FOLIAGE PLANTS. e.g. RUBBER PLANT, PHILODENDRON, ALSO SPIDER PLANT. AVOID FLOWERING PLANTS EXCEPT IMPATIENS

Introduction

When the first settlers arrived in North America, and for many years afterwards, a window full of indoor plants was one of the few simple pleasures pioneer women possessed. Now, millions of people have rediscovered this relaxing and satisfying hobby. The 1960's saw young people suddenly become aware of the year-round joys of indoor gardening, and even very small children are fascinated to watch as plants develop and produce their flowers or new foliage.

Gardening indoors can also be very practical. A beginner can successfully grow a number of vegetables, including tomatoes, lettuce, and radishes, as well as some relatively new types of citrus fruits, and all sorts of herbs. All that's needed is a window greenhouse or an inexpensive, fluorescent light planter. With the same light set-up, home gardeners can save money by starting many annuals, perennials, vegetables, and other outdoor plants from seed.

But probably the most rewarding aspect of growing indoor plants is the natural beauty and freshness that they bring to a home or office. With architects using more glass and open space in their plans for apartments, houses, condominiums, and offices, and with the development of fluorescent and other growth lamps, it is surprisingly easy to grow a wide variety of flowering and foliage plants. Indoor landscaping has, in fact, become a reality.

The term "houseplant" is misleading; it implies that there is a special group of plants which have been developed solely for use indoors. Those labelled as such are merely plants, collected from many parts of the world, which can withstand poor growing conditions. And make no mistake about it, indoors is the worst possible place to grow most plants. The reason is simply that, whether grown for their foliage or their flowers, all green plants require abundant and uniform light in order to thrive. These conditions exist naturally outdoors, but inside they must be simulated through the use of artificial light sources. Of course, there are exceptions to the rule and some foliage plants and a few flowering types will actually grow better with indirect or artificial lighting.

Light

To make indoor plants flourish using only natural light sources, you will have to give careful consideration to where you place them. Outdoors, plants normally receive adequate light from rays of the sun which strike them from all directions. This is not so with a window garden. Most plants will not get sufficient light if they're set on a sill facing north, and they'll only get direct sunlight for part of the day if they're facing east or west. Turning the plants regularly and even moving them between two windows can help to keep the plants thriving.

The majority of flowering plants will require a great deal of direct sunlight, so a large bay or picture window is the ideal location. There are exceptions to this rule as well, however. African Violets, Fibrous Begonias, Reiger Begonias, Gloxinias, Cape Primroses, and some others should either be grown under fluorescent lighting or exposed only to indirect sun, except during the four dark months of the year from November to February, when the sun's rays are weak and slanting.

Most tropical foliage plants need considerably less light than flowering types and will grow well in windows facing north, east and west, or when placed under artificial growth lights. You'll know if your plants are getting sufficient light by their leaves; they will become inactive, turn yellow, and finally fall from the plant if lighting is deficient. The older, more mature leaves will be the first ones affected and, often, when one sees these leaves fall, the first impulse is to give the plant an extra feeding. This is a mistake. When the problem lies in poor light conditions, the leaves will be unable to convert chemical plant food elements such as nitrogen, phosphorus, and potash into usable form. This process of conversion, known as photosynthesis, absolutely demands proper light and is essential to the growth of any plant.

Temperature

Another problem to overcome when growing plants indoors is the high temperature and the extremely dry air in a heated building. While daytime temperatures are not a problem, most homes and offices are too hot in the evening. Even in the tropics, there's a drop of 10°F (5.5°C) or more at night which allows the plants a rest period. With constant high temperatures and lack of moisture, indoor plants will become worn out and sleepy. The majority of them will become leggy and exhibit much less resistance to insect pests and diseases. With flowering plants, any blooms produced will be few and of inferior quality.

A clever way to provide extra humidity is to arrange plants around an aquarium.

While it's not reasonable to expect people to drop the daytime temperatures of their homes and offices simply to accommodate their plants, it is energy efficient and healthy to lower temperatures during the night. In rooms where plants are kept, simply close off radiators and hot air registers or adjust the thermostat to about 60°F (16°C). Plants can even be moved to one particular room at night where the heat is kept low and then returned to their usual place during the day. A small tea cart, such as one would use to transport food from the kitchen, will make moving the plants a simple matter.

Humidity

Plants growing indoors will need a steady supply of fresh, moist air; without it the atmosphere will be drier than the Sahara. If you have a forced air furnace, it's possible to attach a special humidifier which will maintain an adequate level of humidity at all times. Portable, mechanical humidifers are generally available and are equally effective, or you can simply let the kettle steam away in the room twice a day.

Metal or plastic trays filled with gravel and water serve the dual purpose of holding plants and helping to increase humidity. Garden stores also carry plant stands with metal or plastic liners in which a layer of sand, gravel, or plastic chips is placed. Water is then added so that it comes to within 1/2in (1cm) of the bottom of the containers. Plants should never be sitting directly in water as the roots will draw it up and, eventually, rot.

Watering

Incorrect watering is the cause of more trouble for indoor plants than any other factor. Many beginners give daily dribbles of water so that the soil never dries out. The result is a soggy, airless mass in which the plant roots cannot survive. More plants wilt and die through over-watering than through any other cause — they are killed by kindness. While there are a few plants such as Azaleas, Hydrangeas, and Cinerarias which do require daily watering, there are other plants, such as cacti, which have spent hundreds of years learning to do without. Most houseplants fall somewhere in between.

The watering of all indoor plants can be simplified by applying a given amount to each pot at regular intervals. The indoor plant year can be divided into two parts: the eight light months beginning the first of March and the four dark ones commencing the first of November. During the latter months the amount of water needed will be reduced considerably for all indoor plants.

For the majority of tropical foliage plants grown in artificial soil mixtures, a good soaking with room-temperature water twice a week from the first of March to the beginning of November should provide them with the correct amount of water. Watering can be reduced to once a week for the dark months of November, December, January, and February.

The watering of most other indoor plants can also be simplified by applying a given amount to each plant at regular intervals. In homes, apartments, condominiums, and offices, evaporation is just about the same the year round, so once the correct amount is determined, it's easy to repeat. However, watering during the four dark months will need to be cut in half.

Never water to a regular routine. The interval between waterings will vary and depends not only on the plant but on the time of year, the type of soil, the intensity of light, and the amount of humidity in the air. By following a few simple rules you should be able to avoid incorrect watering.

Rules for Watering

1. Observe your plants daily. Keep in mind that if the leaves begin to wilt and droop you have probably allowed the soil to dry out too much. The time to water is when the soil is on the dry side, but before it has dried out completely.

2. Since the majority of roots are in the bottom third of the pot, the water should completely soak the earth ball surrounding the roots. Some water should run out the drainage holes in the bottom of the pot.

3. Avoid using water that is too hot or too cold. It should be room temperature and if you're using tap water, especially for delicate plants, allow it to stand overnight before use. Rainwater or melted snow are ideal for watering your plants.

4. Early morning is the best time to water. Never water in full sun as splashed leaves may become scorched.

5. Poor drainage and placing potted plants in receptacles which hold water around the pot can be very damaging. If your pot is in a receptacle, check a few minutes after watering and discard any excess water.

6. In winter, growth slows down and may even stop. Overwatering must be avoided during this rest period. Until new growth starts in the spring, watering one to three times a month is usually sufficient. During the spring and summer, water will be necessary one to three times a week.

7. As the temperature and light intensity increase, so does the need for water. Plants in small pots and those which have not been repotted for some time need more frequent watering than those in large containers or ones that have been recently transplanted.

Since there are so many variables which determine the correct amount of water for each individual plant, I would recommend making a trial watering for the first few weeks with any new plant. If you're using an unglazed pot (the most common florist's pot and the one I would recommend), a good rule-of-thumb is to apply 4oz (113ml) for a 3in (7.5cm) pot, 6oz (170ml) for a 5in (13cm) pot, and 1pt (.5L) for a 6in (15cm) pot. Plants grown in plastic containers or in glazed pots without drainage holes in the bottom will need one-third to one-half as much

Watering Chart

For purposes of watering, most indoor plants can be divided into three general categories:

* Require the most water — never let the top layer of soil dry out.
** Require regular, moderate watering — keep evenly moist, allow the top one-quarter of soil to dry out between waterings.
***Require the least water — allow the top one-third of soil to dry out between waterings.

GROUP 1 *		GROUP 3 ***
Anthurium	Codiaeum	
Aphelandra	(Croton)	Abutilon
Aralea	Cordyline	(Flowering
Birdsnest Fern	Crossandra	Maple)
Campanula	(Firecracker)	Achimenes
(Bellflower)	Cyclamen	(Cupid's Bower)
Cape Primrose	Dracaena	Agave
Cineraria	Fatsia	(Century Plant)
Cyperus	Ferns	Aloe
(Umbrella Plant)	(except Group 1	Begonia
Fittonia	Ferns)	Beloperone
Fuchsia	Ficus	(Shrimp Plant)
Gloxinia	Fittonia	Bottle Palm
Hydrangea	Flowering Cactus	Bougainvillea
Impatiens	Gynura	Cactus
Maidenhair Fern	(Velvet Plant)	Ceropegia
Maranta	Hedera	(Rosary Plant)
(Arrowroot)	(Ivy)	Cissus
Primula	Hibiscus	(Kangaroo &
Pteris	Jack-in-the-Pulpit	Grape Ivy)
	Monstera	Dieffenbachia
	Oleander	Echeveria
	Palm	Geranium
GROUP 2 **	Passiflora	Herbs
	Pilea	Hoya
African Violet	(Aluminum	(Wax Plant)
Aspidistra	Plant)	Iresine
Baby's Tears	Poinsetta	Jade Plant
Bromeliad	Pothos	Kalanchoe
Caladium	(Devil's Ivy)	Lantana
Calathea	Saxifraga	Norfolk Island
Calla Lily	(Mother of	Pine
Chinese Evergreen	Thousands)	Peperomia
Chrysanthemum	Schefflera	Ponytail Palm
Citrus Trees	(Octopus Tree)	Rochea
Clivia	Spider Plant	Sansevieria
(Kaffir Lily)	Wandering Jew	

water as you would normally use. (It is my opinion, however, that using pots without drainage holes is asking for trouble.) You'll soon be able to observe whether you need to increase or decrease the amount and frequency of watering.

As mentioned before, the majority of the roots of any indoor plant are in the bottom third of the pot. I've always thought it wise to gently knock the plant out of the container the first few times you water. This is easily done by carefully holding it upside down and tapping the rim of the pot on the table. When you do this, you're able to check first-hand the moistness of the soil mixture. If it's not thoroughly wetted through, increase the amount of water used.

Feeding

Unless otherwise noted for a specific plant, the best plan is to feed once a month with a complete indoor plant food, such as an 8-8-8, from the 1st of March until the beginning of November. A complete fertilizer will contain balanced amounts of nitrogen, phosphorus, and potash, plus trace elements: nitrogen promotes the growth of foliage, stems, and branches; phosphorus aids in root growth; and potash acts like vitamins to promote the overall health of the plant. Be sure and follow the manufacturer's directions to the letter when using any plant food.

There's no sense in trying to feed a sick plant; it will not be able to use the food. Neither should you try such home remedies as adding aspirin or tea leaves to the soil as they really have no value at all and if used excessively could even be harmful.

The four dark months of the year — November, December, January, and February — are a time of rest for most indoor plants. They are restoring their energy for the growing season ahead. Flowering plants usually bloom either very feebly at this time of year, or cease to bloom entirely. Exceptions to the rule are Chrysanthemums, Christmas cacti and the Christmas gift plants. These plants have been specially prepared and conditioned to bloom at this time. Low light during the winter also means that most indoor foliage plants will experience very little growth. With these facts in mind, it's foolish to try and stimulate growth or flowering. Much less water is needed, repotting and root disturbance should be avoided, and a feeding at about the beginning of January will be sufficient during the four month rest period.

Care of the Leaves

It's important to keep the leaves of your plants clean. Dust not only spoils the appearance of the foliage, but it blocks the leaf pores so that

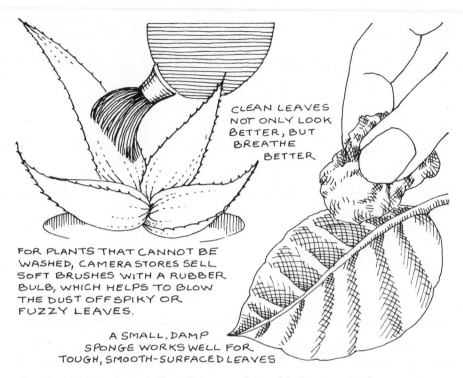

CLEAN LEAVES NOT ONLY LOOK BETTER, BUT BREATHE BETTER

FOR PLANTS THAT CANNOT BE WASHED, CAMERA STORES SELL SOFT BRUSHES WITH A RUBBER BULB, WHICH HELPS TO BLOW THE DUST OFF SPIKY OR FUZZY LEAVES.

A SMALL, DAMP SPONGE WORKS WELL FOR TOUGH, SMOOTH-SURFACED LEAVES

the plant can no longer breathe properly and it forms a surface screen so that the full effect of life-giving light is lost. Dust may also contain plant-damaging chemicals. It's advisable, then, to clean the foliage periodically. Cacti, succulents, and plants with hairy leaves should not be sprayed or washed; instead, use a soft brush to remove the dust.

Even when kept clean, leaves tend to become dull and tired-looking as they age. It's possible, however, to coat the leaves with a water-based material, sold under various trade names, which forms a smooth, glossy finish on the leaves of the plants. This material can either be sprayed on or applied with a piece of cotton wool. The treatment is inexpensive and, in addition to adding to the attractiveness of the plants, will keep the foliage from drying out. When using these commercial fresheners, care should be taken not to apply excessive amounts which might run off the leaves and into the soil as root damage can result. The coating should be applied when the plants are in active growth, with a touch-up job being done about once a month. Don't expect to improve the looks of plants which are not being cared for properly.

Home remedies such as mineral oil, olive oil, cream, or butter should not be used under any circumstances. These will leave a soft coating which attracts dust and, if used in relatively high temperatures, can injure the plants.

Air

One last element which is essential to healthy indoor plants is fresh air; a change of air helps to make the stems stronger and more resistant to disease. Even during the middle of winter, it's a good idea to leave the windows open for five or ten minutes a day; if windows are sealed, you'll have to open a door. In either case, it's very important to make sure there's no chance of plants being caught in a direct draft. In the warmer months of the year, increase daily airing 20 to 30 minutes or more.

Soil Mixtures

Soil taken directly from the garden or field is not usually suitable for growing indoor plants; neither is the rich-looking but poor quality black soil from the woods and forests. The easiest way to obtain a first-class soil mixture for growing indoor plants is to buy one of the specially prepared commercial potting soils that are available everywhere. They come in the form of master mixes, which are suitable for a wide variety of plants, or they can be specifically prepared for such plants as African Violets and Gloxinias.

If you wish to make up your own master mix, use equal parts of top soil, humus, and coarse horticultural or builder's sand. (Coarse plastic chips are now on the market which work just as well as the sand.) For plants such as African Violets, Gloxinias, Fibrous Begonias, and Cape Primroses, your own mixture should consist of two parts top soil, one part humus, and one part sand or plastic chips. In all cases, the humus can be in the form of material from the home garden compost factory, composted cattle manure, peat moss, leaf mold, spent mushroom manure, composted horse or poultry manure that's at least one year old, or ground-up organic bark.

Indoor Plant Hospital

A bathroom with a window or one that is lit by fluorescent or other growth lamps makes a splendid plant hospital due to the high humidity created by frequent baths or showers. An unhealthy specimen given a month or so in the bathroom will usually recover quickly. In larger bathrooms, plants can be used permanently for decorative purposes.

Increasing your Stock from Seed

For a large group of indoor plants, starting from seed is not only a very inexpensive way to obtain new stock, it's much easier than most people think. Many of the better mail order seed catalogues now carry special collections of indoor plant seeds. (Recommended seed firms are listed on the inside back cover.)

If you're a beginner, I'd suggest you start with a package of Coleus seeds. The Coleus is extremely simple to grow and, with any luck at all, one package of seed will produce a dozen or more attractive plants. For the absolute novice, starter kits or seed tapes are also available from seed firms and other gardening sources. Detailed instructions for starting these plants and others are given in the following chapters.

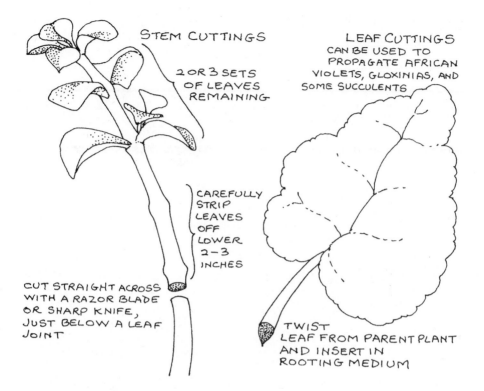

STEM CUTTINGS

2 OR 3 SETS OF LEAVES REMAINING

LEAF CUTTINGS CAN BE USED TO PROPAGATE AFRICAN VIOLETS, GLOXINIAS, AND SOME SUCCULENTS

CAREFULLY STRIP LEAVES OFF LOWER 2-3 INCHES

CUT STRAIGHT ACROSS WITH A RAZOR BLADE OR SHARP KNIFE, JUST BELOW A LEAF JOINT

TWIST LEAF FROM PARENT PLANT AND INSERT IN ROOTING MEDIUM

Taking Cuttings

Taking cuttings is an easy way to increase your plant stock. The best time to do so is in spring or late summer. Choose a healthy stem, cut it just below a joint and clear the leaves from the bottom 2 to 3in (5-7.5cm) of the cutting; there should be two or three sets of leaves left at the top. For those plants which do not have a stem with sets of leaves but a single leaf attached to a main trunk, don't cut the stem from the mother. Instead, twist it from the plant with a gentle turn.

Once you have made your cutting, firmly insert the base into moistened potting soil, vermiculite, or perlite in a 3in (7.5cm) pot. Gently firm the soil around the cutting and give it a small amount of water to eliminate air pockets. Next, put your cutting, pot and all, into a plastic bag and put it in a bright place but not in direct sunlight. When new leaves appear, you'll know that rooting has occurred and the plastic should be removed. If you have used vermiculite or perlite as a rooting medium, repot the new plant in a soil mixture.

Stem cuttings from strong-growing plants such as Philodendrons will often root when simply placed in water. The rooted cuttings may then be transferred to small pots filled with soil.

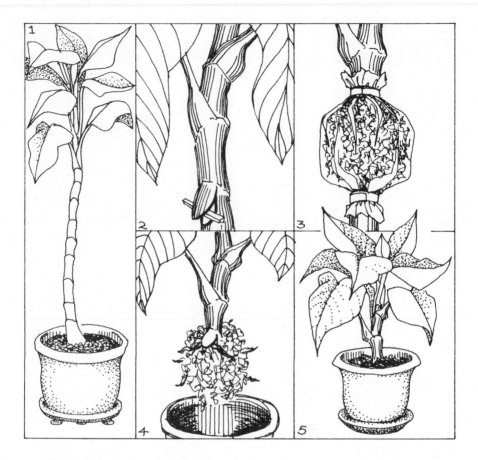

Air-Layering

For large plants such as Dieffenbachias, Dracaenas, Rubber Plants, and large-leaved Philodendrons you can produce new, compact plants by air-layering. An upward cut is made through one-third to one-half of the stem in the place where you want the roots to form, mid-way between old leaf joints. The cut should not be more than 2ft (60cm) below the tip. Open the cut by inserting a toothpick or a matchstick and dust with a little hormone rooting powder, then place a handful of damp peat moss around it, securing the moss with thread. Finish off the air-layer by covering the peat moss with plastic wrap which has been sealed all around with adhesive tape. Keep the moss moist and continue watering the plant as usual. In about three months, roots will have come out of the cut in the stem and into the peat moss. The newly rooted plant can then be cut from the parent and potted up, without removing the peat moss.

INSECT PESTS

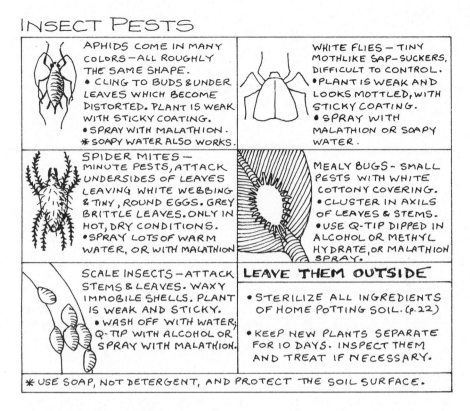

APHIDS COME IN MANY COLORS — ALL ROUGHLY THE SAME SHAPE.
• CLING TO BUDS & UNDER LEAVES WHICH BECOME DISTORTED. PLANT IS WEAK WITH STICKY COATING.
• SPRAY WITH MALATHION.
✳ SOAPY WATER ALSO WORKS.

WHITE FLIES — TINY MOTHLIKE SAP-SUCKERS, DIFFICULT TO CONTROL.
• PLANT IS WEAK AND LOOKS MOTTLED, WITH STICKY COATING.
• SPRAY WITH MALATHION OR SOAPY WATER.

SPIDER MITES — MINUTE PESTS, ATTACK UNDERSIDES OF LEAVES LEAVING WHITE WEBBING & TINY, ROUND EGGS. GREY BRITTLE LEAVES. ONLY IN HOT, DRY CONDITIONS.
• SPRAY LOTS OF WARM WATER, OR WITH MALATHION

MEALY BUGS — SMALL PESTS WITH WHITE COTTONY COVERING.
• CLUSTER IN AXILS OF LEAVES & STEMS.
• USE Q-TIP DIPPED IN ALCOHOL OR METHYL HYDRATE, OR MALATHION SPRAY.

SCALE INSECTS — ATTACK STEMS & LEAVES. WAXY IMMOBILE SHELLS. PLANT IS WEAK AND STICKY.
• WASH OFF WITH WATER, Q-TIP WITH ALCOHOL OR SPRAY WITH MALATHION.

LEAVE THEM OUTSIDE
• STERILIZE ALL INGREDIENTS OF HOME POTTING SOIL. (p. 22)
• KEEP NEW PLANTS SEPARATE FOR 10 DAYS. INSPECT THEM AND TREAT IF NECESSARY.

✳ USE SOAP, NOT DETERGENT, AND PROTECT THE SOIL SURFACE.

Insect Pests and Diseases

Control of insects and diseases that attack indoor plants is not difficult. The number one rule to follow is to put any new plant in an "isolation ward" for ten days before it is placed in with your other plants, no matter whether you purchased the plant or received it from a friend. Examine the plant carefully for evidence of disease or insect problems and, to be on the safe side, spray it with one of the all-purpose indoor plant bombs.

Diseases are less likely to be a problem than insects. Given the correct growing conditions, diseases will seldom become troublesome. However, powdery mildew can be a real scourge on Rieger Begonias and African Violets. It's easily recognized by what appears to be a whitish powder on the leaves and flower parts. Spraying with karathane or sulfur every week will keep it under control. With both fungicides and insecticides, though, be sure to follow the manufacturer's directions to the letter.

Aphids are found in most countries of the world and are one of the worst insects that attack indoor plants. They're no bigger than the head of a pin; some are green in color, others are black, brown, yellow, or pinkish. Aphids suck out the plant juices, causing malformation of the buds, curling of the leaves at the tips, and discolored spots on the foliage. They also damage plants by poisoning them with secretions of their saliva. Spraying every two weeks with one of the indoor plant bombs containing malathion and other chemicals will not only handle aphids, but will control other insects as well.

Spider mites can be a problem where the temperature is high and the humidity low. When spider mites are feeding on your plants, the leaves will turn yellow, become blotched with reddish-brown or white spots, and then die. The underside of the leaves will usually be covered in a fine, white dust which is actually inconspicuous webs and round pearly eggs. Garden stores and nurseries will carry sprays for keeping these mites under control, and there's a special formula for use with African Violets. Frequent syringing of the leaves with a strong stream of warm water will usually control a light infestation.

Mealy bugs often cause trouble for indoor plants. These slow-moving insects congregate in the axils of the leaves and stems and along the main veins. They're covered with a white, waxy material which makes them look like pieces of cotton batting. Coleus, Fuchsi, and all cacti are highly subject to attack. The simplest method of control is to touch each cluster with a small paint brush or "Q" tip, dipped in 50 per cent white alcohol or methyl hydrate. Be careful with the application and make sure none of the chemical hits the stems or leaves. Spraying with room-temperature water, with as much force as the plants will stand without injury, is often effective in eliminating mealy bugs. For serious attacks, use an indoor plant bomb containing malathion.

Scale insects appear as small, flat, oval, or circular spots on the foliage or stems. They develop under the typical, smooth, outer shell and cannot spread from plant to plant by flying. To control a light infestation, gently wash the affected area with room-temperature water, or use a soft brush to loosen the scales. You can also spray the entire plant with an indoor plant bomb containing malathion.

A word on the use of indoor plant bombs. It's a good idea to set the plant in a large cardboard box and direct the mist into it. To avoid burning the plant, be sure and keep the nozzle 12in (30cm) away, but spray both sides of the leaves. The box will help concentrate the spray on the plant and avoid contamination of other parts of the room.

The indoor gardener who makes up his own potting mixtures may have to contend with worms, insect grubs, springtails, and other insects in addition to soil-borne fungus organisms. All of these can be taken care of by sterilizing the soil before use. Just place a pan of moist soil in an oven, heated to 180°F (82°C), for 30 minutes.

African Violets

The most popular flowering indoor plant in North America is the African Violet — over 60 million of these charming plants are sold every year! In the early 1900's, Baron von Saintpaul discovered African Violets in Tanzania (then German East Africa.) The botanical name, *Saintpaulia ionantha*, was given in tribute to von Saintpaul. Even though various European botanic gardens began to grow and distribute them, African Violets did not catch on in those days. Because there was no central heating, it was simply too cold for these plants to flourish.

In 1926, a California nursery introduced the African Violet as the ideal plant for the modern, somewhat overheated home or office. It wasn't long before the Geranium lost its place as number one flowering indoor plant. People had discovered that the African Violet was, in fact, tailor-made to the poor light conditions and high temperatures found indoors and now there are very few homes and offices that don't have at least one of these remarkable plants.

Charming African Violets — the favorite flowering houseplant.

Though not difficult to grow, your African Violet may still fail to thrive unless you attempt to duplicate the conditions it receives in Nature. This is really true for any plant. In the wild — the tropical rain forests of Tanzania — African Violets grow profusely in pockets of woodsy soil among limestone rock, meaning that your soil mixture must be both slightly acid and quite humusy. My own formula is to take a good garden or commercial top soil, add two parts humus, and one part horicultural or builder's sand — the ideal mixture is one that dries out slowly, yet is difficult to saturate. (If you're already succeeding with another formula, follow the cardinal rule of gardening and don't change it. My recommendations are for those who are having problems or for beginners.) A correctly balanced soil mixture is important because, while African Violets will tolerate more moisture than most plants, air must still be able to circulate freely around the roots.

In their natural habitat, African Violets might receive up to 275in (9m) of rain a year and the air is so saturated that these plants can absorb moisture almost as readily through their leaves as through their roots. They'll need to be soaked just as soon as the surface of the soil feels dry to the touch and, unless you're growing them under a fluorescent light set-up covered with plastic, some provision for increasing the amount of moisture in the air is essential. In addition to using mechanical humidification, it helps considerably to place the plants on a tray containing 2in (5cm) of pebbles or gravel and enough water to come within 1/2in (1cm) of the bottom of the pots.

A great deal of nonsense is written about the "correct formula" for fertilizing African Violets, as though feeding a plant were like feeding an animal. However, animals use what they eat directly (digesting proteins, starches, and other elements to create energy) and plants do just the opposite. Their roots take up only the food elements the plants need. From simple chemical elements like nitrogen, phosphorus, and potash, carried through the soil by water, they build more complex substances. The final product becomes food for animals and the cycle is complete.

Unlike animals, plants have no mechanisms for voiding waste or unusable food. More indoor plants are injured by being given too much fertilizer than by not receiving enough. When everything else fails, try cutting the fertilizer application in half — it works wonders with many plants. In fact, African Violets have been kept alive in plain water, with no fertilizer whatsoever, for an entire year. The best plan for correct feeding is to use a soluble, complete fertilizer once a month from the 1st of March until the beginning of November. Plants grown entirely under fluorescent lighting should be fed year-round, once a month, with the same fertilizer.

It's not the way a window faces that spells success with plants but the amount of light they receive. African Violets have been grown quite satisfactorily in windows facing north, east, south, and west — they'll do well anywhere that they receive plenty of diffused light. But keep these plants out of direct sun, except during the four dark months of winter when the slanting rays of the sun will actually encourage growth of leaves and blooms. You'll know if the lighting is correct when the leaves remain horizontal. Too little light and the leaves will stretch up vertically, too much and they will curl around the pot.

One problem that many people have with African Violets is rot which starts at the point where the leaf stem touches the rim of the container. This occurs most often when plants are being grown in clay pots and fed regularly with soluable plant food. The porous clay allows water to rise up and evaporate, leaving a salty residue on the rim. When the tender African Violet stems touch this crust, moisture is drawn out of the stems and a raw spot, or lesion, is created. Eventually, the stem will be destroyed and the leaf will fall off. The easiest solution to this problem is to dip the rim of a clay pot in paraffin before planting, or use a plastic container.

One reliable method of propagating an African Violet is to root a leaf that has 1 to 2in (2.5-5cm) of the stem attached. Insert the cutting 1in (2.5cm) into a mixture of either one part sand and one part vermiculite, or one part sand and one part peat moss. Moisten thoroughly and keep it moist but not soggy at all times. The cutting should be covered with a plastic bag and given plenty of indirect light. In about two months the newly rooted plants will be large enough to pot up.

Growing these plants from seed is also easy and can be done at any time of year. Maintain the seeding medium at 70 to 75°F (21-24°C) during the 20 to 25 day rooting period and don't cover the seeds since they need light to germinate. When they are 1in (2.5cm) high, pot up the seedlings in 3in (7.5cm) containers, using the recommended soil mixture.

Though their natural tendency is to continually produce offshoots, African Violets should be kept to only one plant. Developing plants should be removed from the mother and potted up. A clever way to keep any room alive with the color of African Violets all year is to keep these extra plants in a fluorescent light nursery. You can then work out a rotation system, bringing new plants out at ten day intervals, then returning them to the nursery stock.

A word about potting up plants — African Violets in particular. Setting the crowns too deeply can cause serious problems with stem, or petiole, rot. To determine the correct planting depth you must first be able to recognize the crown of the plant. In the African Violet, it is the swollen portion from which the foliage emerges. The crown should always be set just above the surface of the planting mixture, whether you're potting a newly rooted plant or one secured by dividing the crown of an established plant.

Aspidistras

The Aspidistra is an excellent, almost foolproof indoor plant that comes as close to being indestructible as any indoor plant can be. It will withstand poor growing conditions that few others will tolerate: wide fluctuations in temperature, dry soil, low light, dust, and lack of moisture in the air. Small wonder that its popular name is the Cast Iron Plant.

The Aspidistra comes to our gardens from China, Japan, and the Himalayas. The most familiar type has dark green foliage, but there is a less common variety which features alternating green and cream stripes. The rarity of the variegated Aspidistra is possibly due to the fact that the cream stripes tend to disappear unless the plant is grown in poor soil. With either type, I think the beauty of the Aspidistra is much enhanced by growing it in a cream colored or light green container, rather than a natural clay pot.

The ideal location for the Aspidistra is in a north window, or 3ft (.9m) in from one facing south, east, or west. It will grow successfully in partial sun and under fluorescent lights and growth lamps. Whether it is provided naturally or artificially, relatively little light is needed for the Aspidistra and, while it prefers cool 50 to 55°F (10-13°C) temperatures, this plant will tolerate the normal temperatures found in homes and offices with ease.

You can judge the low light requirements of the Aspidistra by the fact that it has been grown for years under the benches of European greenhouses for the production of leaves alone. These are ideal for making out-of-the-ordinary flower arrangements because they're not only attractive but will remain in a healthy condition for weeks.

Humidity is not a problem; what suits the average person will also suit the Aspidistra. However, I find that misting the leaves daily with warm water always makes for healthier and more attractive foliage.

All indoor plants require water in direct proportion to the amount of light they receive. A good rule-of-thumb for the Aspidistra is to give it a thorough soaking once a week from the beginning of March until the 1st of November. During the winter months, you'll probably only need to water once every two weeks.

It's a good idea to wash the leaves on both sides with a soft sponge or cloth every three or four days to remove the dust that often clogs the

A rare variegated strain of the indestructible Aspidistra.

pores. Again, use room-temperature water and under no circumstances use milk, salad oil, or similar liquids. If you coat the leaves of your Aspidistra with one of the special plant shining products they won't need to be treated with anything but water.

From the beginning of March to the 1st of November, one feeding per month using a soluble, tropical plant food will be sufficient. During the winter, no feeding at all will be required.

The Aspidistra likes to be pot-bound, so it should only be repotted every third year, preferably in March, April, or May. Use a commercial, tropical soil mixture and add one part humus, or take equal parts of sterilized top soil, humus, and coarse builder's or horticultural sand and mix them together.

When you're repotting, you'll probably wish to divide the plant in order to obtain more stock. Although the best time to do this is undoubtedly in the spring, it can be done safely any time of the year. Gently knock the plant out of the container and carefully shake off all the earth from around the roots. At this point you'll find that the leaves can be pulled apart in sections, each one of them having some roots attached. The sections can be potted up singly in 4in (10cm) pots or several can be planted together in a 6in (15cm) container. I've found that a very decorative effect can be achieved by using a rectangular pottery bowel, 2 to 3ft (.6-.9m) long, 2ft (.6m) wide, and 8in (20cm) deep, and planting several Aspidistra sections or small plants in an arrangement.

Cacti

Indoor gardening with cacti can provide many hours of pleasure all year round. Homeowners can move them to the garden during the summer months, while apartment dwellers can put them out on the balcony or patio during the frost-free season. Not only will the plants improve in health, it's surprising how decorative cacti can be. Outdoors, they have the added advantage of being more rigid than other indoor plants and are able to withstand quite strong winds and heavy weather.

The name cactus comes from the Greek word "kaktos", which simply means spiny or prickly plant. Cacti have a rather strange botanical life. Their leafless, fatted stems exhibit the remarkable ability to take up water and store it in their cells. Anyone who's ever grown cacti knows that the skin of these plants is tough with very few deeply sunken pores; this helps to reduce the amount of water given off by the plant. Spines, wool, bristles, and waxy covering also help to shade them from hot sun. Their root systems are shallow and spread out horizontally near the surface of the soil so they're able to absorb whatever rain can penetrate a sun-baked surface.

The cacti we grow indoors belong to a very large family of more than 3,000 specimens which, over many centuries, have adapted themselves to desert life, tropical rain forests, rocky plains, grassy plateaus, and crevices between rocks. Members of the cactus family are found growing only in North, Central and South America. They can be found as far north as the Peace River in Alberta and as far south as Patagonia in Argentina.

The most distinctive characteristic of most cacti is their ability to store large quantities of water for use in time of drought. This means that constant watering by the indoor gardener will surely result in their death. The amount of water required by cacti is determined by the amount of usable light they receive. However, if the plants are watered infrequently at all times, particularly during the period of active growth from the 1st of March to the beginning of November, they will remain dormant. The best way to water cacti is to give each plant a thorough soaking and then allow the top 1in (2.5cm) of soil to dry before watering again. A good rule of thumb would be to give them a good watering once a week for the eight light months beginning in March and then, during the dark months of winter when the cacti are dormant, water just enough to keep the hair and feeder roots from drying out. From November through February, I find that once a month is sufficient. I also recommend watering on a sunny day when the sunshine will help to draw the water up through the roots to the rest of the plant.

Where cacti grow in the desert or other outdoor locations, they naturally receive plenty of sunshine and fresh air. Keep this in mind when growing them indoors. It's preferable to choose a window facing south, but one facing east or west would be satisfactory and cacti will also do well under fluorescent or other growth lamps. Maximum indoor temperatures of 72 to 75°F (22-24°C) are ideal, but you should drop the temperature at night to 60°F (16°C). It's particularly important to create a cooler atmosphere at night during the dormant period which will last from the beginning of November to the 1st of March.

Despite the fact that many varieties of cacti originate in the desert, a well-drained, rich soil mixture is needed for them to grow well indoors. Commercial soil mixtures for cacti are generally available but for those who prefer to make their own, a proven formula is to mix equal parts of top soil, composted cattle manure or material from the home garden compost factory, peat moss, and coarse horticultural or builder's sand. There are certain cacti that are water-sensitive and for these the amount of sand should be increased and the amount of peat moss decreased.

Every two weeks during the growing season, feed the cacti when you water, using a soluble, complete plant food that is low in nitrogen, high in phosphorus and potash. Garden stores and nurseries will carry plant foods specially prepared for cacti. No feeding at all will be required in the dormant period.

The only pest that seems to attack cacti is the mealy bug which, as mentioned in the section on Insect Pests and Diseases, is a soft-bodied insect that appears as a cottony ball on the body of the plant. A simple method of control is to touch each cluster with a small paint brush or "Q" tip which has been dipped in 50 per cent white alcohol or methyl hydrate. Make sure the chemicals do not come in contact with the skin of the cactus. An alternative method of dealing with mealy bugs is to gently wash them off with warm water. You'll probably need to do this three or four times, a week apart, so that successive new hatchings will also be eliminated.

Small cacti and succulents create very attractive desert arrangements in a dish garden, but it's a serious mistake to plant Begonias or other tropical plants in the same container. The water requirements are completely different and, sooner or later, something will die.

Six of the easiest cacti to grow are: Owl's Eyes (*Mammillaria*

Each of the 3,000 members of the cactus family is unique.

parkinsonii), Prickly Pear (*Opuntia microdasys*), Crown Cactus (*Rubtia kepperiana*), Bishop's Cap (*Astrophytum capricorne*), Rattail Cactus (*Aporocactus flagelliformis*), and Pin Cushion (*Mammillaria bocosana*).

Cacti are readily grown from seed obtained from the major mail order seed firms. In sowing the seed, fill a 5 to 6in (13-15cm) clay or plastic pot with a half-and-half mixture of potting soil and coarse builder's or horticultural sand. Firm down with the fingers and level, leaving 1/2in (1cm) between the surface of the soil and the rim of the pot for watering purposes. Scatter the seeds evenly over the soil mixture and cover lightly with a fine soil mixture. Place in full light, where the temperature will be from 70 to 80°F (21-27°C). Give a good soaking with room-temperature water and cover with a plastic bag. When the seedlings start to appear, remove the plastic. Transplant to 3in (7.5cm) clay or plastic pots just as soon as the seedlings are 1in (2.5cm) or so high, using the soil mixture recommended earlier for cacti.

Caladium

Sierra Leone, just north of the Equator on the west coast of Africa, and the Amazon area of Brazil have provided indoor gardeners with the delightful Caladium, grown for its fancy, beautifully marked, and multi-colored foliage which is carried on 15in (38cm) plants.

In 1821, the Royal Horticultural Society of London, England sent out still another Scottish gardener to collect exotic plants in tropical countries. George Don had become foreman of the famous Chelsea Physic Garden on the banks of the Thames at the ripe old age of 23. On

Almost translucent, the Caladium is fragile and delicately veined.

April Fool's Day 1822, while climbing the Sugar Loaf mountains of Sierra Leone, he recorded finding gloriously colored Caladiums, Ixias, and Salvias.

Caladiums will flourish in fairly dense shade where few other plants will grow well, making them ideal for growing indoors in the low light conditions found there. The large, arrow-shaped leaves are widely variegated in colors of green, red, pink, cream, white, and fascinating combinations of the same. This tuberous plant, hailing from tropical climes, belongs to the Arum family which gave our temperate woods and gardens the Jack-in-the-Pulpit and also the Calla Lily.

Whether you grow the Caladium as an indoor foliage plant, in a container on a shady balcony, or in a shaded spot in the garden, it's important to realize that the colorful leaves grow from tubers in much the same way as Dahlias and cannot be grown the year round. The plants can be in active growth for as long as nine months but following this they must have a three month rest before starting to grow again. It will take two months from the time you start the tubers growing until you have plants large enough to be attractive indoors or for moving outdoors to the balcony or garden. Those used indoors can be started off anytime they're available from garden stores but for outdoor use we need to time their growth so they can be moved outside once warm weather has arrived to stay at the beginning of June.

A plastic seedling flat or bulb pan is the best type of container to use for starting the tubers. Partially fill the container with one of the following potting composts: dampened leafmold, a half-and-half mixture of peat moss and sand, or material from the home garden compost factory. (Leafmold is generally available from garden centers and nurseries.) Keep in mind that the roots grow from the top of the tubers, so be sure to cover them with 2in (5cm) of the dampened potting mixture.

Give the containers a location in full light but out of direct sunlight, where the temperature can vary from 70°F (21°C) to as high as 85°F (29°C). The tubers will also root well under fluorescent and other growth lamps. Water sparingly with room-temperature water until the roots and plants are growing vigorously.

When the roots are 2in (5cm) long, it's time to move the Caladiums to 6in (18cm) pots. Use the same commercial soil mixture as you would for African Violets or indoor, tropical foliage plants. If you prefer to make up your own mixture, use three parts leafmold or material from the home garden compost factory, one part builder's or horticultural sand, and one part top soil. After repotting give a good soaking with room-temperature water and continue to keep the plants in a full light location or under fluorescent and other growth lamps, but out of direct sunlight. At the same time, provide a warm and humid atmosphere. Increase the humidity reading on your hygrometer so it's as close as possible to 50 per cent. Remember, we wrote earlier that Caladiums originally came from the tropical rain forests of the Amazon River and Sierra Leone in west Africa. With this in mind, it pays to syringe both sides of the foliage twice a day with room-temperature water. This recommendation also applies to Caladiums grown in containers outdoors. For those in the garden, a light sprinkling with the hose once a day will do wonders for them.

Give a feeding every two weeks with a soluble, tropical plant or fish emulsion fertilizer from the time the leaves begin to grow vigorously until they start to fade in the early fall. You will probably discover that the leaves will be quite small in the beginning with their stems seeming to be abnormally long. Not to worry, this condition soon changes.

As the days become noticeably shorter in the early autumn the tubers will begin to lose their leaves when grown outdoors. Indoors, they'll also start to lose their foliage after they've been in the pots for an eight to nine month period. This is your cue to gradually reduce the watering and, when all the leaves have dropped away, stop it completely. Dig up the tubers planted in the garden or remove those grown in containers. Dry them off, dust with a combination insecticide-fungicide, and store each one in an individual paper bag for the vital three month period. Try and keep the temperature in the storage period from 50 to 60°F (10-16°C). Anytime after the rest period is over the tubers can be started off again.

Don't be penny wise and pound foolish when selecting Caladium tubers, buy the large ones averaging to 2 to 2-1/2in (5-6.5cm) in diameter.

Mail order bulbs and seed catalogues list numerous separate colors. Try **Frieda** whose many solid red leaves have a delightful green border. Those of **Blaze** are red with spectacular scarlet ribs and a striking light green edge. **Pink Beauty**, a pleasing soft pink on a dark green background with rose ribs, is lovely in any setting. The foliage of **Sunburst** is a deep emerald green with numerous blotches and a large center of oriental red which extends out each vein and looks like an exploding sun. One of the strongest growers is **Mrs. W.B. Haldeman**, whose leaves are a luscious, rich watermelon-pink with green ribs and borders.

Cape Primroses

Cape Primroses (*Streptocarpus*) are a magnificent group of indoor plants which are not widely grown in North America, despite the fact that they're "kissing cousins" to the African Violet and require exactly the same growing conditions. Originating in South Africa, these plants produce exciting, long-lasting, trumpet-shaped blossoms from May to October. The foliage is also very attractive, having a graceful curving shape and a velvety texture. Anyone who is successful with African Violets will have no trouble with the Cape Primrose.

Seeds are generally available from mail order seed catalogues and can be sown during any month of the year. The seeding medium should be kept at 75°F (24°C), using bottom heat, and germination will take 15 to 20 days. The fine seeds should not be covered as they need light to germinate. When the young seedlings are about 1in (2.5cm) high, move them to 3in (7.5cm) pots and use the same soil mixture as recommended for African Violets.

Cape Primroses do very well when grown in shallow containers such as bulb pans and will thrive in a fluorescent light garden or on a shaded patio or balcony during the summer. Generally speaking, the indirect light required for African Violets is also necessary for these plants.

Some strains of the Cape Primrose that I particularly recommend are the giant flowering hybrids, specially bred to produce blooms of unusually large size. They average 3 to 3-1/2in (7.5-8.5cm) across and are so ruffled and fluted that they resemble Orchids. The plants reach 10in (25cm) high and should be grown in 6in (15cm) pots. The **Nymph** series produces exceptional quantities of 2 to 2-1/2in (5-6cm) blooms on compact 8in (17.5cm) plants and should be grown in 4in (10cm) containers. **Massen's White** has pure white blooms with an attractive touch of cream in the center, while **Rosita** features deep pink blooms and glossy green leaves. You'll also like **Constant Nymph,** with its delightful blue blossoms and long, glossy green foliage. Perhaps the most attractive of all, however, is **Kolibri**, with its compact plants and free-blooming capability. The top two petals of each flower will be a soft pink and the three bottom ones a pinkish-red with distinctive markings.

[*Opposite page*] *Cape Primroses — the symmetry of velvet foliage and pastel blooms.*

Carnivorous Plants

There's a group of unusual plants in the world which are correctly termed carnivorous — they actually attract, catch, and eat insects to obtain nourishment. This ability allows the plants to obtain nutrients which are not available to them from the nitrogen-deficient soil or moss in which they grow naturally. Over thousands of years, these plants have developed methods of catching their meals which vary from drowning their prey to trapping the insects in leafy cages.

There are several species of carnivorous plants, available from garden stores, nurseries, and mail order seed catalogues, which can either be grown in terrariums or used as ordinary houseplants. They also make wonderful subjects for growing in school classrooms and can provide intriguing science projects for teachers and students. Indoor gardeners will welcome the chance to grow something different and to observe them at close quarters.

Many North Americans are familiar with the Pitcher Plant (*Sarracenia*) since it's found growing wild in many areas. As the common name implies, the plants are shaped like pitchers, or vases. Rain collects inside the pitchers and additional moisture is brought up from the moist soil and moss in which the plants grow. Some reach only 4 to 5in (10-13cm) in height, while others may grow to 15in (38cm).

Insects are attracted to a sweet substance which is secreted by the glands of the plants and also by the bright coloration of the pitchers. Once they have entered the pitchers, the insects discover that the sharp spines and hairs lining the inside make it almost impossible to get out. Eventually the insect drops from exhaustion into the liquid inside the pitcher. Digestive enzymes dissolve the body tissues which are then absorbed by the plant.

Deceptive coloring helps Pitcher Plants trap their meals. Some, such as the Hooded Trumpet (*Sarracenia minor*) and the Sweet Trumpet (*Sarracenia rubra Walters*), develop almost translucent spots on the top rear of the pitchers. Insects easily enter the hollow pitchers through the colorful opening, but when they try to fly out again they're deceived by the light colored spots, fly into them and tumble down the hollow stem. Escape is virtually impossible.

The Miniature Huntsman's Horn develops several slender pitchers varying from 4 to 8in (10-20cm) in height, with the tops marked with reddish veins. This type and the brightly colored Northern Pitcher Plants are excellent selections with which to begin a collection.

Another easy to grow, fly-catching plant is the Sundew. In sunlight, the sticky substance on the tiny tendrils glistens beautifully. The tendrils are clustered on the tip of each arm that radiates from the Sundew's center. Although the plant itself is generally only about 1in (2.5cm) in diameter, the strength of its tentacles can be compared to that of an octopus in their ability to hold the victim. Insects attracted to the odor of the glistening red Sundews have only to touch the sticky tentacles to become caught. As the captive struggles, other tentacles bend to touch the insect, secreting more of the protein-digesting enzymes.

Nature has also endowed the Cobra Lily with the means of catching its own food. The forked tongue is covered with honey glands which attract its prey. Once inside the hood, downward pointing hairs prevent the insect from crawling out. The digestive liquids are found in the base of the plant.

Studies have revealed that the Venus Fly Trap has a high degree of sensitivity, comparable to a very primitive nervous system. The plant grows from a tuberous bulb with narrow arms radiating from the center. On the end of each arm is a leafy trap, hinged in the center, with several tiny trigger hairs on each lobe. When an insect is attracted to the trap and touches two of the hairs, the trap is sprung quickly and decisively. As the victim struggles, the trap is stimulated to produce a fluid which drowns the insect in an airtight chamber. The Venus Fly Trap seems almost to be intelligent. If the trigger hairs are purposely stimulated, the trap will snap shut. However, if it finds itself without a meal, it will reopen within 24 hours.

For the indoor gardener who wants to start growing carnivorous plants, the best thing to do is to use a terrarium and select Pitcher Plants, Venus Fly Traps, and Sundews. Sundews need moisture but should not be overly wet, so locate them in the highest part of the terrarium for best results. All of these plants thrive in sunlight or under growth lamps, in warm temperatures and high humidity. They need to be starved in order to function properly so never give them any fertilizer; they should also be grown in a poor soil mixture. Try a mixture of six parts sphagnum moss, two parts builder's or horticultural sand, and one part composted cattle manure or material from the home garden compost factory. I doubt if you will be able to find a suitable soil sold commercially.

To water carnivorous plants never use tap water. While water from the tap is fine for the majority of indoor plants, provided it's allowed to stand overnight, it contains trace elements which will restrict the appetite of carnivorous varieties.

Chinese Evergreens

The Chinese Evergreen (*Aglaonema commutatum*) of Southeast Asia is my nomination for the most foolproof indoor plant. While it grows best in bright but diffuse sunlight, it will also do well in the corners of rooms, away from the windows. It will flourish in a north window, under fluorescent lights, or 3 to 4ft (.9-1.2m) in from south, east, and west windows during the summer months. In the winter, it can be placed in any window.

Chinese Evergreens grow very well in water gardens and are ideal plants for the beginner to hydroponics. When grown in pots, they like the soil to be moist at all times and in good light locations will need watering twice a week from the beginning of March until the 1st of November. In low light locations, a good soaking with warm water every two weeks will be sufficient. As with all tropical foliage plants, providing mechanical humidification or placing the plants on a tray of pebbles and water will help to keep the air surrounding them from being too dry. The leaves should be washed daily on both sides to keep them at their healthiest. During the winter, watering can be cut back to every five or six days in well-lit locations, and much less in poorly lit ones.

During the growing months, beginning in March, feed the Chinese Evergreen once every two weeks. Use a soluble, tropical plant food such as an 8-8-8 when you water. From November through February, no plant food will be needed.

As mentioned before, Chinese Evergreens require a growing medium which retains a great deal of moisture. I suggest using one of the commercial African Violet soils and adding one part humus, or make up your own using two parts sphagnum moss, one part top soil, and one part coarse builder's or horticultural sand. For every gallon (4.5L) of growing medium, I usually add a heaping tablespoon (15ml) of complete garden fertilizer, such as a 4-12-8 or a 10-10-10. You'll need to repot these plants every second year in March or April and additional plants may be obtained at this time by division.

In July, small white flowers may appear but the Chinese Evergreen is really grown for the beauty of its foliage and for its ability to survive

low light conditions that few other indoor plants would tolerate. *Aglacomina pictum* is a particular class of Chinese Evergreen which, when small, makes an ideal plant for growing in terrariums, Wardian cases, and bottle or dish gardens.

Cissus

Lack of light is one of the biggest problems indoor gardeners must overcome. Obviously, the best way to deal with this is to select plants which don't mind low light conditions. Just such a plant is the Kangaroo Ivy from Australia. Its botanical name, *Cissus antarctica,* comes from the Greek "Kissos", meaning Ivy.

The foliage of the Kangaroo Ivy is leathery and dark green, deeply notched around its edges and an attractive dark brown on the underside. The leaves normally grow 4 to 6in (10-15cm) long, but there's also a dwarf variety whose leaves seldom exceed 3in (7.5cm) in length. The leaves, flowers, and tendrils of the Kangaroo Ivy are very similar to grape vines and the first plant explorers mistook it for a member of this family. But it is, in fact, a true ivy.

The best situation for Kangaroo Ivy is in about 3ft (.9m) from windows facing south, east, and west, or on a ledge facing north. They also grow very well under fluorescent lighting.

These plants should be watered moderately during the growing season from the 1st of March until the beginning of November, and the surface of the earth should be allowed to become fairly dry before giving them a good soaking with room-temperature water. During the dark months of the year, a watering every seven to ten days should be sufficient. As with any indoor plant, the less light received, the less water is required.

This type of ivy in particular is easy to overfeed. Plants fresh from the garden store need no feeding for the first three months and from then on should be fed only once a month with a complete, tropical plant food. During the winter, they should not be fed at all.

Every other February, the Kangaroo Ivy will need repotting using one of the commercial, tropical plant soil mixtures to which you've added one part humus. If you wish to make up your own mixture, it should consist of equal parts of sterilized top soil, humus, and coarse builder's or horticultural sand.

As with all smooth-leaved, indoor plants, the Kangaroo Ivy will benefit from a daily syringing on both sides of the leaves. It will also pay to stand the plants in a tray filled with 2in (5cm) of pebbles and just enough water so that the bottoms of the containers will be 1/2in (1cm) above the level of the water.

Citrus Trees

One of the best of the tropical fruits now widely available to the indoor or balcony gardener is the Calamondin Orange (*Citrus mitis*), originally found growing in the Philippines. It has also been called the Panama or Philippine Orange. No special treatment is required and with correct light, water, fertilizer, and soil mixture this plant can provide years of generous flowers and edible fruits.

These miniature oranges measure an inch (2.5cm) or more in diameter and are usually green when you receive the plants from the garden store or florist shop. They'll gradually turn orange-yellow to orange in color. When fully ripe they can be eaten like tangerines, although the pulp is slightly more tart than an orange or a tangerine, and they can also be used to flavor beverages and other foods. Juice from fruits that are not fully ripe makes a most delicious whiskey sour or a delectable marmalade, and they can be freely substituted for lemons and limes.

Plants are upright, compact, slow-growing dwarf trees. Like the other members of the citrus family, the small, scented, waxy white blooms appear off and on throughout the year, often at the same time as the miniature fruits. However, the peak flowering time begins in February and lasts until the end of the summer.

The Calamondin Orange will only flower and fruit well when it is grown in a fully sunny window or under fluorescent and other growth lamps.

Temperature during the day should be 68 to 72°F (20-22°C) but should be lowered to 60°F (16°C) at night for best results. Beginning in February, give a good soaking twice a week with room-temperature water, cutting back to once every five days in November. It also pays to syringe the leaves on both sides with warm water every day. Spray the foliage every two weeks with an indoor plant insecticide, containing malathion, to control scale, red spiders, and other insects.

Give the plants a feeding every two weeks from the beginning of March until the 1st of September using one of the soluble, tropical plant foods. Make sure you follow the manufacturer's directions to the letter; don't add extra plant food to the water in the vain hope that if a little will do a good job, a lot will do much better.

Your orange plant should grow in its original container for at least two years. May is the time to move it to a larger pot. Use one of the commercial, tropical soil mixtures or make up your own consisting of equal parts of top soil, peat moss, material from the home garden compost factory, and coarse builder's or horticultural sand. When the plants start becoming leggy, they'll need pruning back - do this during March, April, and May.

By June you can sink your orange plant up to its rim in a sunny but sheltered spot in the garden, or place it in a sunny location on the balcony or patio. Continue to feed as you would indoors. Containers of oranges on the balcony or patio will need a good soaking every other day while those buried in garden soil will need watering only once a week.

In the autumn, move the plants indoors before the first frost. Don't worry if most of the old leaves drop off; this is caused by the change in temperature and humidity. With good care, your plant will be covered with silky green leaves again within three or four weeks.

The Calamondin Orange likes a humidity reading indoors of 30 per cent on the hygrometer. It's a good idea to set this plant in a metal or plastic tray filled with pebbles and water, keeping the bottom of the pot 1/2in (1cm) above the level of the water at all times.

The seeds of the oranges and grapefruits we eat or the lemons we use for cooking will produce small trees 2 to 3ft (.6-.9m) high in a surprisingly short length of time. When the trees reach this height most people start expecting blossoms and fruits to appear in the not too distant future. Eventually, when none appear, they blame themselves for neglect. Nothing could be further from the truth; fruits only develop on specially grafted trees which can be ordered from the garden store or nursery.

Despite the lack of fruits, trees grown from citrus seeds have very attractive, shiny green leaves and are among our better, long-life indoor plants. Selecting the seeds, sowing them in a pot, watching them germinate and grow, can all be fascinating fun for any member of the family but most of all for small children.

To sow the seeds you'll need a 6in (18cm) clay or plastic container, a plastic bag, a commercial, tropical plant soil mixture, and a few pieces of broken clay pots, barbecue charcoal or the new plastic drainage pieces. Make a start by placing 1in (2.5cm) of the drainage material in the bottom of the pot and then add the soil. Fill the pot to the rim and then firm it down with the finger tips. After firming, the surface of the soil mixture should be 3/4in (1.9cm) below the rim for watering purposes.

Wash the citrus seed thoroughly and plant three of them to each container. Make a hole 1/2in (1cm) deep and 1in (2.5cm) wide in the soil

Kangaroo Ivy is a versatile hanging or trailing plant. *Calamondin Oranges bear edible fruit.*

mixture. Insert the seeds, cover with soil, and soak the potting mixture thoroughly with room-temperature water.

To prevent the soil from drying out too quickly, cover the pot with a plastic bag. Until the seeds begin to germinate, the container can be kept in any location where the temperature is around 68 to 72°F (20-22°C) and out of direct sunlight. After germination, move to a sunny, well-lit location, under fluorescent lights, or other growth lamps. If more than one seed germinates, as will frequently happen, separate the seedlings and replant in three weeks time using a 6in (18cm) pot and a tropical plant soil mixture.

Once the new plants are 3 to 4in (7.5-10cm) high, begin to feed them once a month with one of the soluble, complete, tropical plant foods such as an 8-8-8. A daily syringing of both sides of the leaves will keep the pores free of dust and dirt and will raise the humidity of the air around the plants.

In June, when the warm, sunny weather has arrived to stay, the young trees should be moved to a sunny location in the garden or on a balcony or patio. Over the summer months they'll develop renewed vigor in the ideal growing conditions found outdoors and it will also give the wood a chance to ripen. September is the time to move the citrus trees back to their proper indoor location.

How well does this work? I recently repotted the citrus trees of an old family friend and it had been started off in this manner more than 50 years ago.

Coleus

Originally found growing on the island of Java, the Coleus is a familiar garden annual. Because it does so well in shaded spots outdoors, it's also ideal for growing inside. The Coleus is a truly spectacular plant, grown for its multi-colored foliage rather than its insignificant blooms. The color range is infinite and combines chartreuse, bronze, gold, copper, yellow, pink, red, green, purple, and white. Many new varieties have recently been introduced whose leaves may be smooth, edged, fringed, toothed like oak leaves, or wrinkled. Depending on the variety, the plants vary in height from 6 to 36in (15-90cm). For indoor use, it's best to choose those that grow 15in (38cm) tall or less.

Even for beginners, growing the Coleus from seed is extremely simple. Any pot that is 4 to 5in (10-13cm) in diameter will do for sowing the seeds, though I prefer to use a shallow bulb pan measuring 5 to 6in (13-15cm) across and 4in (10cm) deep. The best soil mixture is one of the commercial African Violet or tropical plant soils. No fertilizer will be required at this stage, since almost any soil mixture you choose will contain sufficient plant food to sustain the tiny seedlings as they germinate and for the first three or four weeks of their lives.

Fill your container to the rim with the soil mixture and firm it around the edges. After levelling, the surface of the seeding mixture should be 1/2 to 1in (1-2.5cm) below the rim of the pot so that you can water without spillage. Scatter the seeds on top of the soil and don't cover them — they'll need light to germinate. After a gentle soaking with warm water, cover the container with a plastic bag or a pane of glass, then place it in a well-lit location, out of direct sunlight. It will take ten days to two weeks for the seedlings to appear. Usually, no more water will be required until the first seedlings are up and the glass or plastic has been removed. If you use a pane of glass, you won't need to water again as long as you can see beads of water collecting on its surface and dripping back down onto the seeds. Once the first seedlings appear, the glass or plastic should be removed immediately. I find that it's wise to check for germination eight days after sowing.

The seedlings should only be moved to 3in (7.5cm) pots after the leaves have developed real color. Some of the last plants to show color will have the loveliest and brightest pastel tints. When the seedlings have made a second pair of leaves, all of the color will have started to

The leaves of the Coleus may be smooth, edged, fringed, toothed or wrinkled, and the color range is infinite.

show and they can be moved to their containers. A good tropical plant mixture or one prepared for African Violets should be used for this first repotting. After the job is done, give each plant one-third of a cupful of special starter solution to get the plants off to a fast start and overcome transplanting shock.

Your Coleus will need plenty of light and water, and make sure that the air surrounding the plant is kept moist, especially in the winter. To keep the shape and color of Coleus attractive, they should not be allowed to get too old as they will gradually lose the brightness of their colors. Also, to encourage bushy growth, the tips should be pinched back frequently. For the best results, it's a good idea to take cuttings about three times a year. These will root easily in water or a mixture of sand and peat and ensure a steady supply of new, healthy-looking plants.

Cordylines

The Cordyline family has given us two delightful indoor plants: the Hawaiian Ti Plant (*Cordyline terminalis*) and the New Zealand Grass Palm (*Cordyline australis*). The Hawaiian Ti Plant is the most dramatic of the two, with its striking foliage colored in vivid reds, pinks, and cream variations. In its natural habitat, the Hawaiian Ti Plant often grows 10ft (3m) tall and the attractive, broad leaves are used for thatching huts, for cattle fodder, and for making the well-known grass skirts. Flower arrangers find them useful as the leaves of the Hawaiian Ti are easily shaped by gentle molding to take on unusual forms.

In 1777 David Nelson, a young English botanist, was sailing with Captain Cook on the H.M.S. Discovery when they visited New Zealand. On a trip inland he found the New Zealand Grass Palm. It doesn't have the attractive color variations in its leaves but relies on overall gracefulness for its charm.

Both of these plants will require the same treatment. First, they will need to be located where there's plenty of light: in a north window the year round; in any window during the winter; and in about 3ft (.9m) from a window facing south, east, or west for the summer months.

Secondly, I doubt if you'll be successful in growing either plant unless your home or office has some form of mechanical humidification. Most certainly, the plants should be set on a plastic or metal tray filled with water to within 1/2in (1cm) of the bottom of the pots. A daily spritzing with warm water is a must. From the 1st of March until the beginning of November, they will need a good soaking every third or fourth day. During the winter, cut back to watering once a week.

A soluble, complete, tropical plant food should be used every two weeks during the growing months, and no feeding at all will be required during the winter. Both Cordylines are vigorous growers and will need repotting every other year in March or April. Use one of the commercial, tropical plant soils to which you've added one part humus. If you wish to make your own mixture, combine equal parts of top soil, humus, and coarse horticultural or builder's sand.

It's possible, though difficult, to start these plants from seed and you can sow during any month of the year. You'll find, however, that started plants are widely available, as are bits of stems, called logs,

Vivid red, pink and cream variations in the Hawaiian Ti enhance its dramatic effect.

which have been waxed to keep them from drying out. These logs should be split lengthwise and the cut side placed on a mixture of sand and vermiculite. A deep casserole dish or mixing bowl will make a satisfactory container, and the medium should be kept moist. Cover it with a pane of glass or a piece of plastic and place the dish in a location where a temperature of 75°F (24°C) can be maintained; it may be necessary to use some bottom heat.

In a short time, buds will form and roots will start to penetrate the vermiculite/sand mixture. At that point, either select the strongest buds, or split the log into as many pieces as you have buds, making sure each piece has roots. Pot them up in regular containers, using a commercial, tropical potting soil to which you've added one part humus. You can also make your own mixture by combining equal parts of top soil, humus, and coarse builder's or horticultural sand.

47

Crotons

I doubt if there's another indoor plant whose leaves are so beautifully colored and unique in appearance as those of the Croton (*Codiaeum*). Many centuries ago it was brought from Malaya to Greece, where the world's first florist shops originated. The Greeks used the bright foliage to make crowning wreaths for victorious armies and the winners of sporting contests.

Unlike many indoor plants that require a 10°F (5.5°C) drop in temperature at night, the Croton will thrive in continuous day and night temperatures of 68 to 72°F (20-22°C) or better. For this reason, it makes a better than average indoor plant and in very warm climates is an excellent garden shrub.

The foliage of the Croton exhibits an almost endless variety of color combinations, including green and pink, reddish-gold, greenish-yellow, yellow and brown, and many others. The more light and sunshine you're able to provide, the more colorful they'll become. For this reason, you'll need to supplement the natural sunlight in winter with fluorescent or other growth lamps. Without additional light, even with high levels of sunshine, the foliage will tend to be a yellow-green rather than the bolder and more spectacular reds and oranges.

The leaves can also vary widely in shape. One of the most unusual varieties, *C. spirali,* has twisted leaves and branches resembling the corkscrew willow. The green foliage is dotted with blotches of red and yellow.

Crotons are fast growers and in a hobby greenhouse, a conservatory, or in the wild, they will become tall shrubs. When used as indoor plants, the best plan is to keep them 2 to 3ft (.6-.9m) high by pinching them back in February when the days are becoming noticeably longer.

From the middle of June until the beginning of September, Crotons can be moved outdoors to foundation beds and borders or around the patio. The plants should be kept in their containers and buried to the rim in the earth. Several plants massed together in a sunny location will create a fine show of color. On a balcony or patio they should be placed in a full sun location. Again, the warmer the summer and the brighter the sunshine, the more colorful the leaves. Placing the Crotons outdoors in the summer will invigorate them and make them stronger for the indoor season.

Since the Malayan climate is not only very warm for most of the year but also very humid, success with Crotons will require adding moisture to the air. In a dry atmosphere this plant is extremely susceptible to the pesky little mite commonly called the red spider.

Even with mechanical humidification, the plants should be placed on trays filled with 2in (5cm) of gravel or pebbles and the level of water in the trays should be maintained within 1/2in (1cm) of the bottom of the containers so that it will continually evaporate into the air.

The humid conditions necessary for Crotons can be further simulated by syringing the leaves twice a day with warm water. I like to keep a plant syringe or atomizer close by the Crotons and other smooth-leaved, tropical plants and spray them whenever I think of it.

Crotons need a soil mixture that's rich and fibrous, containing plenty of humus. Material from the home garden compost factory, peat moss, composted cattle manure, or leaf mold are all excellent. A good soil mixture should contain equal parts of humus, top soil, and coarse horticultural or builder's sand. Alternatively, you can use one of the commercial, tropical plant soils to which you've added one part humus.

Drainage is important with all plants and excellent drainage can be ensured by placing a 1in (2.5cm) layer of broken charcoal on top of the two or three pieces of clay pot which are normally used for this purpose.

During the growing season, your Crotons will need a good soaking with lukewarm water every three days, reducing this to every five days during the winter months. Beginning in March, feed them twice a month with one of the soluble, complete, tropical plant foods such as an 8-8-8.

Crotons will need repotting every second year, using the soil mixture mentioned earlier, and new plants are easily propagated from cuttings or produced from seed. With any vigorous growing tropical plant such as this, it's wise to keep a supply of young plants coming along. Select shoots that are about 4in (10cm) long and set them in a clay or plastic pot filled with a mixture of half sand and half peat. Dust the cuttings with one of the hormone rooting powders before inserting them into the pot. Rooting will occur much more readily if the container is covered with a plastic bag to maintain the level of humidity and heat. Move the cuttings to individual 3in (7.5cm) pots just as soon as a ball of roots has formed.

Seeds may be sown indoors anytime during the year, provided the medium is kept at between 70 and 80°F (21-27°C). This means that some bottom heat will be required. You'll have to be a little patient; germination takes about 30 days. When the young seedlings are 2in (5cm) high, move them to 3in (7.5cm) pots filled with the recommended soil mixture. Gradually move the Crotons to larger containers as they grow.

Dieffenbachias

One of the very best plants for growing in our dry, well-heated homes, apartments, condominiums, and offices is the Dieffenbachia or Dumb Cane, originally found in Brazil. The Dieffenbachias are a fine group of colorful and decorative indoor plants which are widely used for their striking and handsome foliage which is elliptical to heart-shaped. The broad green leaves are dramatically accentuated with liberal splashes or blotches of creamy white on the upper surface.

I've always found the Dieffenbachia to be comparatively foolproof and ideal for growing in most homes and offices because it doesn't require bright light to grow well and is quite adaptable to warm air.

From the beginning of March until the 1st of November, Dieffenbachias can be placed in a north window or in about 3ft (.9m) from windows facing in other directions. They will also respond particularly well to fluorescent light and other growth lamps. During the dark months, any window will do.

The Dieffenbachia is one of the few plants that is difficult to overwater, but coming from the tropical jungles of Brazil means that it requires a high level of humidity. Aside from mechanical humidifiers, one of the best ways of providing moisture in the air is to take a deep bowl and lower a saucer upside down in the center. Add sufficient water to bring the bottom of the saucer just above the water level. Place the Dieffenbachia on this small island and the water will gradually evaporate into the surrounding air and maintain the needed humidity. The water level should be kept constant and at no time should the bottom of the container come in direct contact with the water.

This plant is one of a small group which will benefit from a repotting every March or April. Use a commercial, tropical potting soil to which you've added one part humus. To make up your own, use equal parts of top soil, humus, and coarse horticultural or builder's sand.

From March to November, give the Dieffenbachia a good soaking every third day with warm water. In winter, watering once a week should be sufficient. Spray the plants daily on both sides of the leaves. Every second week, while you water, use a soluble, complete plant food such as an 8-8-8. During the winter months, you won't need to feed at all and you should water less because the low light conditions

The Croton exhibits an endless variety of color combinations, while the Dieffenbachia's handsome foliage [rear] is accentuated by ivory markings.

Even though the Red-margined Dracaena resembles a Palm, it is just as sturdy as the broad-leaved Dracaena fragrans.

mean that any new leaves which are formed will tend to remain small and it's best to discourage them.

As the plants become older, the lower leaves will fall off. Be assured that you're probably not doing anything wrong; it's just the nature of the Dieffenbachia. Leggy specimens can be rejuvenated by a little ruthlessness; cut the stem back to 6in (15cm) and new growth will appear in very little time.

Dracaenas

In 1822 the Royal Horticultural Society chose George Don, a young Scottish horticulturist and a foreman at the Chelsea Physic Garden, to hunt for plants on three continents and to scour the island-studded oceans and seas between. In South Africa he found the Dracaena which was destined to become one of our most popular and easy-to-grow indoor plants. While there are a dozen varieties which make excellent low-light plants, my favorite is the Red-margined Dracaena. Also known as the Dragon Lily or the Madagascar Dragon Tree, it resembles a plant commonly called the Spanish Dagger. In fact, the two are closely related and are members of the Lily family. Unlike the Spanish Dagger, however, the sword-shaped leaves of the Red-margined Dracaena are soft, bend easily, and are not prickly.

The Dracaena, or Dragon Plant, is a tough plant which will grow well in both sun and shade. I find that it's one of those plants which will do particularly well on the balcony or patio from the beginning of June until the middle of September, or later in areas where the autumn is mild.

The branches of the Red-margined Dracaena tend to twist and bend, creating a very picturesque effect, and the plant often grows at an angle. The crowns of the red-edged leaves constantly renew themselves so that this plant will last for many years. The Dracaena grows more slowly than many tropical plants, however, so it pays to buy a fairly large one at the outset.

These plants will do best if the soil is kept barely moist. A good soaking once a week should be sufficient during the light months beginning in March, and watering once every ten days should be enough in the winter. Once a week, put your Dracaena in the bathtub and give it a shower, letting the warm water gently wash off the leaves.

Dracaenas will require only two feedings a year: one at the beginning of March and the other at the beginning of September. Use a soluble, complete, indoor plant food such as an 8-8-8.

Flowering Cacti

There is a special group of cacti which have been bred to flower at Christmas, Thanksgiving, or at Easter. These indoor plants have enjoyed a renewed wave of popularity owing to the creation of new and better varieties.

The most common mistake in caring for these plants is to treat them like desert cacti. They are not plants of semi-arid countries but originate in the upland regions of Brazil. Unlike true cacti they need the growing medium kept constantly moist, but not dripping wet.

Any of these flowering cacti need a soil which is considerably richer than you would use for other cacti. The ideal soil mixture is one consisting of equal parts top soil, humus, and coarse builder's or horticultural sand. Ground up pieces of plastic, relatively new to the marketplace, can be used with excellent results in place of the sand. As for humus, I prefer to use one of the composted cattle manures or material from my home garden compost factory. To each quart (1.1L) of this mixture, add 1T (15ml) of a complete indoor plant food.

After the warm weather arrives and there's no danger of frost, the best location for these plants is in some sheltered and partially shaded spot in the garden, out of direct sun. Bury the pots to the rim in the soil and see that they receive a good soaking with warm water every four or five days to keep the medium moist.

Indoors, these cacti like a bright light situation. Keep them out of direct sunlight except in the winter months when they can be moved to the sunniest window of your home. All three of these plants will grow well under fluorescent lights.

The flowering cacti will benefit from a daily syringing from the time the buds start to form until blooms begin to open. They are also like the majority of indoor plants and relish plenty of moisture in the surrounding air. Use a humidifier or a plant tray filled with sand, gravel, or plastic pieces and enough water to maintain the level at 1/2in (1cm) below the bottom of the container.

The most common complaint I receive about these cacti is that the plants form plenty of buds which either drop off before they open or, at best, only develop a few blooms. This can be caused by overwatering, exposure to cold drafts, lack of potash in the soil, or a location too close to a hot air register or radiator.

If you've had your plants outside during the summer, the first two weeks of September is the time to move them indoors. Place them in a good light situation, but out of direct sun. Like Chrysanthemums or Poinsettas, they will need a period of long nights and short days to encourage blooming. Beginning in the first week of October and for the next eight weeks, place the plants in a dark cupboard with absolutely no light, from 5:00 p.m. until 8:00 a.m. During this two month period, the plants are semi-dormant giving them a rest period which is vital to their setting buds. A light watering every two weeks will be all that's required, just enough to keep the leaves from shrivelling. Cacti that bloom at Thanksgiving will need to enter their rest period in the last week of August, while those that bloom at Easter will need to go into semi-dormancy in early January. Keep the temperature between 60 and 65°F (16-18°C) during this period.

At the end of the dormancy period, resume the normal twice a week watering which will last until the end of the flowering season. At that time, water once a week until the new shoots begin to appear, then go back to watering twice a week.

Flowering cacti that are left in the same container year after year without having their soil renewed will stop flowering sooner or later. You can tell if the soil has become too poor if you notice the leaves starting to turn yellow. I like to repot every two years. I also make it a practice to replace the top inch (2.5cm) of soil in the container each January, or immediately after the flowering period has ended.

In potting up any of these plants make sure you don't firm the soil mixture too hard around the roots. During their active growing season they'll be given plenty of water, but it should run freely through the growing medium. To further help this process, put an inch (2.5cm) of broken clay pot, or some of the new plastic chips, in the bottom of the container before starting to add the soil.

Cuttings are easily rooted in moist sand and peat or vermiculite during the first two weeks of April. Use healthy pieces of stem, 3in (7.5cm) long. Dip the ends in a hormone rooting powder just before planting. During the rooting period, cover the containers with a plastic bag and place in a well-lit location, out of direct sunlight. Once the new roots are 1/2in (1cm) in length, pot up the new plants in 3in (7.5cm) clay, plastic, or peat-fibre pots using the soil mixture recommended previously.

The misty web of an Asparagus Fern, the ruffled form of a Boston Fern, delicate Maidenhairs, and a fluted Birdsnest create natural beauty in an indoor arrangement.

Ferns

A fern is one of the very best plants to grow where light conditions are only fair; there's hardly a wood, forest, jungle, or desert anywhere in the world which doesn't have some ferns growing in it. Three hundred million years ago they covered the earth with an unbelievable abundance.

Ferns are almost always found growing in damp situations where the air surrounding them contains an abundance of moisture, with the exception of the species which inhabit the desert regions. The real key to success with ferns in the indoor garden, then, is to make sure that the air contains plenty of moisture at all times. Most failures with ferns can be attributed to a dry atmosphere.

The surest and most reliable method of increasing the amount of moisture in the air is to use either a portable humidifier or one that is attached to a forced air furnace. Since humidity is such a vital factor in growing ferns, I strongly advise setting them in trays of a suitable length and width to fit a window or fluorescent light set-up. Most garden stores and nurseries carry a stock of trays that have a minimum depth of 2in (5cm) and are capable of holding water, though a small baking pan or pottery bowl will do nicely for one or two plants.

It might also pay to buy a hygrometer which gives accurate readings of the humidity, with subsequent benefits to indoor plants. For the majority of ferns you grow, a reading of 50 on the hygrometer is ideal.

Ferns will also appreciate a daily syringing with water at room temperature. (Special indoor plant syringes are inexpensive and available everywhere.) The Maidenhair Fern is the only variety we grow indoors whose delicate foliage is harmed by spraying in this manner.

The soil mixture for ferns should contain plenty of humus. It's easiest to use one of the commercial, tropical plant soils and add one part humus. If you wish to make your own, the mixture should consist of equal parts of top soil, humus, and coarse horticultural or builder's sand.

Ferns don't need repotting nearly as often as most other indoor plants. Older, mature plants can be kept in the same container for several years, provided you renew an inch (2.5cm) or so of the soil at the top of the pot each year. This can be done at any time, though it's best carried out in March, just as the days start to lengthen.

Feeding three times a year with a complete soluble, tropical plant food will be sufficient for ferns. The first should be given at the beginning of March, another in June, and the last in September.

While your ferns won't require direct sun, they do like plenty of light. A window facing north or a location in about 3 or 4ft (.9-1.2m) from a window facing east or west are ideal locations. During the winter, they can be placed in any window. Ferns will also grow well under fluorescent or growth lamps.

Because new types of Boston Ferns have been developed which are more attractive and have a built-in ability to withstand the relatively high heat and poor growing conditions found indoors, they are becoming increasingly popular. Other graceful varieties grown indoors are the Staghorn Fern, the Bird's Nest Fern, the Maidenhair Fern, the Spider or Table Fern, the Holly Fern, the Asplenium or Mother Fern, and the Squirrel's Foot Fern.

Ficus

The members of the Ficus family are exotic, tropical plants originally found growing over a very wide section of the warm parts of the world. They've come to our indoor gardens from such far away places as Africa, Australia, Burma, China, India, the East Indies, and even from the southern part of Japan.

None of them would have been found growing in grandmother's

The taller the Weeping Fig [opposite page] grows, the more graceful it becomes and the Ficus pumila [above] makes a lovely trailing plant.

home. Without central heating, houses then were much too cold for these quick-growing tropical plants. Fortunately, today's homes, apartments, condominiums, and offices are kept in the 68 to 72°F (20-22°C) range, providing the warm growth conditions required by members of the Ficus family.

The India Rubber Plant [*Ficus elastica*] and its cousin the Fiddle Leaf Fig [*Ficus pandurata*] are probably the best known and easiest to grow of this group of exotic plants. Both have large and abundant leaves which are Nature's way of enabling them to make the most of the poor light conditions and abundant moisture of the tropical jungles where they grow wild. Because of their natural habitat, they are ideally suited to the warm temperatures found in today's homes and offices.

In dry air conditions, the big, 18in (45cm) leaves of these plants will continue to function as they were programmed to by Nature, and give off moisture much faster than it can be replaced. Unfortunately, watering more abundantly or more often is not the answer when growing them indoors. The plants are not able to take up water through their fine hair roots and transfer it quickly enough to the leaves. This means that you're keeping the earth continuously wet, oxygen is unable to circulate freely, and eventually the roots will begin to rot. You'll know if your Ficus is receiving too much water when the bottom leaves become brown and start dropping from the plant. The only solution to this problem is to raise the humidity in the air surrounding the plants. There are several ways of accomplishing this, which we have discussed before. You can either install a mechanical humidifier, or use a portable model. Syringing the leaves daily with warm water will also help raise the humidity and keep the pores of the leaves from being clogged by dust. Spraying the leaves is so important to the India Rubber Plant, the Fiddle Leaf Fig, and all smooth-leaved, indoor plants that it will pay to make it part of your daily routine.

The relative humidity in the room should be somewhere between 40 and 50 per cent, which is ideal for both plants and human beings. If you don't have a mechanical humidifier, the daily syringing of the leaves should be combined with setting the plants in trays deep enough to contain 2in (5cm) of pebbles or coarse gravel. Keep the water level almost to the top of the pebbles, but make certain the bottom of the container is not sitting in the water.

The Ficus plants will go dormant in the winter, although they may not appear to do so. They require a rest period and it's important to lower the temperature to 60°F (16°C) during the evening hours, if at all possible. A good soaking with warm water once a week should be enough at this time; it's far less harmful to underwater during the winter than it is to overwater.

From the beginning of March until the 1st of November the plants will probably need a good soaking once every four days. Again, the big leaves will benefit from being sponged on both sides once a week.

During the growing period, give the plants a feeding every two weeks with one of the tropical, complete plant foods such as an 8-8-8. Follow the manufacturer's directions to the letter and don't overfeed.

Both of these plants will need a location where there's plenty of bright light, but keep them out of direct sun. They can be in a north window the year round, in any window during the dark months of November, December, January, and February, and 3ft (.9m) in from a window facing south, east, or west for the remainder of the year. They also grow very well under fluorescent or other growth lights.

The Fiddle Leaf Fig and the India Rubber Plant will need repotting every second year and the best time to do this is during March or April. You can use one of the commercial, tropical plant soil mixtures to which you've added one part humus but I prefer to make up my own using equal parts of top soil, humus, and horticultural or builder's sand. Leaf mold, composted cattle manure, or material from the home garden compost factory are the best forms of humus for this purpose.

These fugitives from the tropics grow so vigorously that it isn't many years before they are too tall for the average house or apartment. For this reason, it's wise to keep a succession of young plants coming along, either purchased from the plant store or, in the case of the India Rubber Plant and the Weeping Fig [*Ficus benjamina*], they can be grown from seed sown any month of the year. The seed should be left uncovered in order to germinate and seeding containers will need bottom heat to keep the medium at 70 to 80°F (21-27°C). Germination will take from 15 to 20 days. When the seedlings are 2in (5cm) high, move them to 3in (7.5cm) pots and use one of the commercial, tropical plant soils to which you've added one part humus. As the plants continue to grow, move them to larger containers.

Once a Fiddle Leaf Fig or an India Rubber Plant becomes too tall, it's easy to create a new plant by propagating it through air layering, as discussed at the beginning of the book. Make the cut 2in (5cm) long and 10in (25cm) below the growing tip. After rooting occurs, pot up the new plant using a clay or plastic container which is 2in (5cm) larger than the diameter of the root ball. Use one of the commercial, tropical plant soil mixtures or make up one of your own consisting of equal parts top soil, humus, and coarse horticultural or builder's sand. Give it a good soaking with warm water.

In recent years, the *Ficus benjamina* (Weeping Fig or Airport Plant) has become one of the most popular indoor plants. It's undoubtedly the most graceful of all the figs and the taller it grows, the more graceful it becomes. Its leaves are quite small, averaging about 4in (10cm) in length, and come to a sharp point at the end. They're carried on drooping branches and the young foliage is colored a bright, light green which becomes glossy and dark as it matures. The Weeping Fig is

The India Rubber is a strong and imposing Ficus.

grown in the same way as the India Rubber Plant or the Fiddle Leaf Fig. Great care must be taken in the dark months of the winter not to overwater. This is a time of rest for the plant and giving it too much water will mean that the leaves drop quite freely.

I find that the Weeping Fig may be moved to a shaded spot in the garden at the beginning of June, as long as there's plenty of indirect light, and returned indoors about the middle of September. There will undoubtedly be some dropping of leaves when it goes outdoors and when it comes back inside.

The *Ficus benjamina* can also be grown quite easily from seed, sown indoors any month of the year. Seeds should be left uncovered as light is needed for germination and the container will need some bottom heat to keep the seeding medium at between 70 to 80°F (21-27°C). It will take anywhere from 15 to 20 days for seedlings to appear and when they reach 2in (5cm) in height, move them to 3in (7.5cm) pots using one of the tropical plant soils to which you've added one part humus. Set them in larger containers when the small pots become filled with roots.

Gardenias

There are a number of species of Gardenia found growing wild in Mexico and Brazil, but the tropical, flowering plant we grow indoors is the *Gardenia jasmoides* which was originally found in China by William Kerr. Kerr was a young Scottish gardener, sent abroad in 1803 by Sir Joseph Banks, the head of Kew Gardens in London, England. Kerr was the first botanist to hunt for plants in China for a lengthy period of time. During his first year in Canton, he sent some specimens of the Gardenia back to Kew Gardens. It, and other plants, travelled to England on the East India Company's ship the Henry Addington. It's a wonder that any of the specimens survived since, in those days, the voyage could take as long as six months.

Gardenias can be frustrating. Many indoor gardeners buy a lovely green plant in full bud only to have the buds drop off one by one before any of them bloom. Even if the Gardenia is actually coaxed into bloom, it seems even more difficult to make it bloom again. Let me assure you that Gardenias can be made to flower regularly, provided some essential conditions are met.

First of all, the best location is a window facing south, with sheer drapes between the Gardenia and the window pane. No matter where they're situated, Gardenias need a minimum of direct sunlight. For this reason, fluorescent lighting is ideal; a three-tube, daylight, white fluorescent light set-up, with the plants placed 2ft (.6m) from the tubes will be sufficient for them to flower. You can be certain, though, that if Gardenias don't receive at least four hours of sunlight daily, or 12 hours a day of fluorescent light, all you'll ever get is green leaves.

Let's assume that you've successfully encouraged the Gardenia to flower for the first time, and you're wondering how to get it to do so again. The blooming period usually ends in the middle of May and the plant enters a vegetative, or green leaf, period. Go on keeping the earth constantly moist, but not saturated. Gardenias are one of the very few plants that need to be watered a little every day. They also need to be grown in an acid soil.

In many parts of North America the water is alkaline, as opposed to acid. To counteract this, you must water Gardenias once a month with a solution made up of 1/2oz (14g) of iron sulfate, dissolved in a gallon (4.5L) of water. Iron sulfate is easily obtained from your local druggist.

Around the middle of June, the plants should be pruned back to 10in (25cm) stubs; the vegetative period will continue until the beginning of October. The first three weeks of October are vital to your Gardenia if it's to set buds and bloom again. You must make this a short day and long night period. The plants should be in the sunlight or under fluorescent lighting from early morning until dusk and then moved to a dark cupboard or other completely light-free location where the temperature can be lowered to 65°F (18°C). At the end of the three week period, make sure there's at least four hours of sun a day or 12 hours of fluorescent lighting.

Gardenias will need to be fed once a month the year round with a complete tropical plant food, such as an 8-8-8. In the winter months, be sure and drop the temperature to 60°F (16°C) during the evening.

Because of the dryness of the air in the average home or office, Gardenias will drop their buds if there isn't some form of artificial humidification. You'll need to use a portable humidifier or one attached to the forced air furnace, or place the plants in a tray or pan filled with pebbles and enough water to keep the level 1/2in (1cm) below the bottom of the containers. You can also lower a saucer upside down into the center of a water-filled pottery or plastic container. Again, the bottom of the saucer should always be 1/2in (1cm) above the water with the Gardenia being placed on the bottom of the saucer. Whatever method you use, the water will evaporate into the air around the plant. It's particularly important to syringe both sides of the leaves with warm water every day without fail.

You'll need to repot Gardenias every other June using one of the commercial, tropical plant soils to which you've added one part humus. To make up your own, use equal parts of sterilized top soil, humus, and builder's or horticultural sand.

Gloxinias

In the latter part of the 18th century, plant hunter botanists started fanning out all over the world seeking new plants and by the early 1800's Europe was experiencing a "golden age" in horticulture. It was truly an age of discovery and during the 1700's the colorful and free-blooming Gloxinia [*Sinningia*] was found growing in Brazil and brought to Germany. It's named after P.B. Gloxyn of Strasbourg, who was the first man to grow Gloxinias outside of Brazil.

Despite its early discovery, the Gloxinia didn't come into its own until central heating became common. It's one of a small group of indoor plants that thrive in the warm temperatures of the modern home or office and I believe that Gloxinias will become more popular still with the increased use of fluorescent lighting for indoor gardens.

Breeders have been doing a lot of work with these plants in recent years and we now have both single and double blooming Gloxinias. The magnificent coloring of their velvety-textured flowers, the attractive foliage, and the ease with which they may be grown, make Gloxinias one of the most exciting indoor, blooming plants. It's always a puzzle to me why they are not more widely grown.

Patience, careful watering and feeding are the keys to growing Gardenias successfully. They need a loose, humusy growing mixture consisting of one part leaf mold, one part top soil, one part horticultural sand. Leaf mold is packaged commercially, but if it's not available, any of the following will make satisfactory substitutes: composted cattle manure, material from the home garden compost factory, peat moss, or ground-up organic bark. Perhaps the best mixture for the beginner to use would be one of the commercial African Violet soils to which is added one part leaf mold.

Commercial flower growers are able to bring Gloxinias into bloom every month of the year with the ideal growing conditions found in their greenhouses. For the home gardener, though, the best plan is to start Gardenia tubers any time from the end of December until the end of April. The tubers produced in Belgium are excellent and not as expensive as some of the specialty strains. I'd make a start with these and then as you gain experience try some of the more costly varieties.

It's vital that the Gloxinia be encouraged to develop a first-class root system; without it you'll achieve little in the way of bloom. When you purchase your tubers be certain to obtain two sizes of pots. To start them off, select clay or plastic pots in the 3in (7.5cm) size which is usually just large enough to hold the tubers. Later on, when these first containers are filled with roots, the plants should be moved to 5 or 6in (13-15cm) pots.

In starting off the tubers, barely cover them with the rooting mixture and immediately after potting give them a good soaking with warm water. You won't need to water again for as long as seven to ten days. Overwatering at this stage, when the roots are just starting to develop, usually means failure to bloom. Some weeks later the plants will develop flowering buds to the point where they're about to open and then, much to their owner's exasperation, they will drop off. Place the pots in full light out of direct sun, or under fluorescent lights, and keep night temperatures at 60 to 70°F (16-21°C). In just a few days, the puckered brown tubers will start to send out small, hairy leaves which look like tiny mouse ears. Not long afterward, the plant will begin to grow vigorously and soon the 3in (7.5cm) pots will be filled with masses of roots. This is the time to move them to larger pots.

The newly rooted Gloxinias should be set in the containers so that the top of the tuber is 1in (2.5cm) below the surface of the growing mixture. At this point, you should still be going easy on the water, keeping the mixture moist but not saturated. After four or five leaves have developed, the plants will need plenty of moisture. A good soaking with warm water, twice a week, should be about right. This is also the correct time to start feeding Gloxinias regularly, using a complete, tropical plant food every two weeks. An 8-8-8 fertilizer will be appropriate.

One of the main requirements of the Gloxinia is having an abundance of moisture in the air at all times. A portable, mechanical humidifier, or one attached to the forced air furnace, is a must for these plants. It will also pay to keep Gloxinias in a tray filled with pebbles and water maintained at 1/2in (1cm) below the bottom of the containers.

Three months from the time you start off the tubers, you'll be seeing the first buds open. Plants sown at the beginning of January will give you blooms by the first week in April and if you make several plantings three weeks apart, you can have flowering Gloxinias until early autumn.

The more experienced indoor gardener can have a great deal of fun and save considerable money by growing Gloxinias from seed. It takes only six to eight months from seeding until the new plants begin to flower and seeds can be sown any month of the year. Don't cover them as the seeds need light to germinate and the containers will need some bottom heat to maintain the temperature at 70 to 75°F (21-24°C). In 15 to 20 days the first little seedlings will start to appear and when they're an inch (2.5cm) or more high, move them to 3in (7.5cm) pots using the

Romantic Gloxinias combine warm colors and soft textures.

same growing mixture as you would use for the tubers.

Once the Gloxinias have finished flowering, gradually cut down on the amount of water you give them until the leaves turn brown and fall away from the tubers. Store the plants, in their containers, in a dry, cool location over 50°F (10°C). Late in the fall, start checking the pots weekly for the reappearance of the puckered, brown leaves. As soon as this happens, repot as before in a fresh soil mixture and return to a well-lit window or a fluorescent light set-up.

Hoyas

Queensland, Australia has provided our indoor gardens with the exotic and sweetly perfumed Wax Plant [*Hoya*], an outstanding climbing and flowering vine. It will produce clusters of star-shaped, pink, red, or white blossoms from May until September. The vines themselves are semi-succulent and rope-like, with thick, shiny, dark green leaves which grow about 3in (7.5cm) long.

These plants look best when they're trained on a trellis (simply a loop of stiff wire running around the sides and top of a window.) They're also easily trained for indoor topiary. The *Hoya carnosa* and the *Hoya bella*, in particular, are especially good plants for hanging baskets. The *Hoya bella* is a dwarf variety which grows only 18in (45cm).

All of the Wax Plants are fussy about being disturbed. You may find the buds dropping before the flowers open unless you learn how to handle them. The main reason the buds drop has been found to be frequent movement of the containers. I suggest you make a mark at the front of the container so that you'll always be able to put it back in exactly the same position if you are forced to move it at all.

An east or west window, where the temperature doesn't vary as much as one facing south, would seem to be the best location for any Hoya. If you must use a south window, protect the plants from the sun by keeping a sheer drape between the plant and the window or by moving it 2 to 3ft (.9-1.6m) into the room. However, during the four dark months beginning in November, plants located in east and west windows will do better if they're moved to a south window and given direct light. All of the Hoyas will thrive under fluorescent light or growth lamps.

Wax Plants relish a humid atmosphere and a daily misting on all sides of the leaves and the stems. To achieve the 30 to 40 per cent humidity level, some form of mechanical humidification will be required. A good soaking twice a week during the growing period will be necessary, as well as a feeding every two weeks with a soluble, complete, tropical plant food. In the winter, cut back the watering to once every week or ten days, letting the earth dry out between waterings. The plants should not be fed at all during this period.

With most flowering plants, the advice is to remove blooms as they fade to encourage the development of more flowers. With Wax Plants, don't cut off the dead blossoms; let them drop from the plants naturally. New flowers will appear on the same spurs in the following year.

At the beginning, the Hoya is not a fast grower. One of the main requirements for getting these plants to bloom well is to keep them pot-bound. When roots surround the inside of the pot, most plants need repotting but the Wax Plant will be in its glory.

When you must repot, do it in April and use a rich soil mixture. Choose a commercial, tropical soil to which you've added one part humus. If you make up your own, use equal parts top soil, humus, and coarse horticultural or builder's sand. To each bushel (35L) of this mixture, add 1/2pt (284ml) of a granular, complete, tropical plant fertilizer.

New plants are easily propagated from mature stems, cut in the summer. Dust the cuttings with one of the hormone rooting powders and then insert them into a mixture of sand and peat. Give a gentle soaking with warm water and cover the cutting with a plastic pot. When the roots are 1 to 1-1/2in (2-3.5cm) long, move them to 3in (7.5cm) clay or plastic pots and use the same soil mixture as recommended earlier.

Wax Plants can also be grown from seed, started any season. The seeding medium should be kept at 70-75°F (21-24°C) during the germination period, so you'll need some bottom heat. The first seedlings will make their appearance in 10 to 15 days. When they're 1in (2.5cm) or so high, move them to 3in (7.5cm) pots

This gracefully trailing Hoya is adorned by artistic, pastel markings.

Impatiens

One of the most difficult problems faced by the indoor gardener is finding plants that will bloom well in windows facing north or where tall buildings nearby obstruct the light. In such circumstances, the Impatiens is an excellent plant to grow. It is both an outdoor and indoor plant, originally found growing in East Africa on the island of Zanzibar. There's also another type, recently introduced, which comes from New Guinea and has extra large blooms. The name Impatiens refers to the seed pods which, when ripe, will scatter their seeds on all sides at the slightest pressure.

When growing Impatiens from seed they should be treated in the same way as the Coleus. The seeds are left uncovered as they need light for germination and it takes 15 to 20 days for seedlings to appear. They may be sown at any time of year.

I find the small and medium-sized Impatiens to be the best for growing indoors. Brightly colored, single flowers and some doubles, are borne on bushy plants. The color range varies from rose, pink, red, and white to terra cotta, lavender, and tangerine.

The Impatiens will thrive in normal indoor temperatures of 68 to 72°F (20-22°C) and it's also one of the few plants that won't require additional moisture in the air surrounding it.

You can usually purchase started plants from garden centers during most months of the year. Alternatively, plants that are growing well in shaded spots in the garden, or under similar light conditions on the balcony or patio, can be pinched back to 6in (15cm) stubs in early October and potted up. Use 8in (20cm) containers and one of the commercial African Violet or tropical plant soil mixtures. By the end of November, these stubs will have produced vigorous new growth and will be bursting into bloom once again.

During the winter, you can safely keep your Impatiens in windows facing in any direction. For the rest of the year, the best spot is in a north window or 3ft (.9m) in from those facing east, west, or south. The Impatiens is ideal for growing in artificial lighting.

Like the Coleus, the Impatiens will need a good soaking with room-temperature water every three or four days, easing off to once a week during the dark months of November, December, January, and February. Feed these plants once a month with a soluble, complete, tropical plant food such as an 8-8-8 and mist the leaves once a day with warm water.

Narcissus

How would you like to have a bowl of fragrant, snowy-white flowers perpetually enhancing the beauty of your living room, library, kitchen, or dinner table? All you need do is go to your nearest garden store or bulb dealer in the fall and buy some Paperwhite Narcissus bulbs.

Growing these delightful and eye-catching bulbs indoors is just about the easiest gardening job in the world. Even the least experienced gardener or a small child can expect 100 per cent success on their very first try. Paperwhites are also the answer for the would-be gardener who lives in a small apartment and is very limited in what he can grow.

Many gardening books and articles will insist that Paperwhites must be treated like Tulips, Hyacinths, Daffodils, and other spring-flowering bulbs and given a period in the dark in order for them to bloom well. I'm happy to report, after conducting numerous trials over the last few years, that this is in no way true. In fact, Paperwhites given a two or three week period in the dark after potting will always produce leggy stems. On the other hand, the best thing to do is to put the bulbs in a container and immediately place them in your brightest window. This will keep the stems short and stocky and help to prevent the plants from falling over toward the end of their flowering period.

Paperwhites originally came to our gardens from nurseries in southern France, but interest in producing bulbs there waned and Israeli growers took over. They are now providing the best quality bulbs we've seen in years.

As with all bulbs to be forced indoors, always buy the highest quality and the firmest specimens available. Forcing any bulb into bloom out of season is asking a lot, and you'll need the best possible bulbs for the job. I suggest that you buy at least a dozen Paperwhites so that, by starting off four bulbs at a time, ten days to two weeks apart, you'll have fresh blooms coming along for a four to six week period. Anyone wishing to create an exciting display over the Christmas season should buy 25 bulbs at least and start them off in soil in a seedling flat. Just as they come into bud, move them to suitable containers.

Under normal circumstances, most indoor gardeners will use a shallow pottery or plastic bowl 8 to 10in (20-25cm) in diameter. It should be deep enough to hold sufficient amounts of pebbles and gravel

ADD PEBBLES TO COVER LOWER HALF OF BULBS FOR SUPPORT

FILL WITH WATER TO JUST BELOW BASE OF BULBS

2 INCHES OF PEBBLES BELOW BASE OF BULBS

so that, when the bulbs are set in place on top of them, there will be 2in (5cm) of space between the base of the bulb and the bottom of the bowl. This amount of room is necessary to allow for the good root development which is so essential to production of quality blooms.

Once you've added the stones or gravel to the container, set the bulbs in place leaving 2in (5cm) between them. Then add water to within 1/2in (1cm) of the bottom of the bulbs. You'll find that the water level will gradually drop over the next two or three days as it's taken up by the bulbs or lost through evaporation. Once the level drops to just below the bottom of the bulbs, keep it constant — if the base of the Paperwhite is always sitting in water, rotting invariably occurs. Next, move the bowl to the sunniest window and wait for buds to appear. Just as soon as the buds begin to open, the bowl should be removed from the direct sunlight and placed in indirect light so as to lengthen the flowering period as much as possible.

Soleil d'Or, a yellow form of the Narcissus and closely resembling the Paperwhite, can also be grown in water and pebbles. These are the famous daffodils which flourish outdoors in Bermuda and on the Isles of Scilly, off the coast of England.

You'll need the same type of bowl and pebble arrangement as for Paperwhites, but the Soleil d'Or need to be kept in a dark, cool place for a two week period before they are exposed to the sun. (A good place for this is in the refrigerator.) In every other respect, they are treated like Paperwhites. Both of these bulbs should be discarded when the flowering period is over.

Norfolk Island Pine

Given the current housing trend, it won't be long until there are more people living in apartments and condominiums than there are occupying homes. Such a situation may cause problems around Christmas time because many apartment and condominium complexes ban the use of live Christmas trees as they are potential fire hazards. It's also true that there is an increasing ecological awareness, and many people object to cutting down a live tree just to use it as decoration for a few weeks. On the other hand, artificial trees lack the charm of the traditional spruce or pine.

Fortunately, a simple solution to all of these problems is the Norfolk Island Pine (*Araucaria exelsa*). This charming, tropical evergreen is an ideal, miniature substitute for the Scotch Pine or Balsam Fir I always bought when my children were small. Now, we spend every Christmas in Bermuda and continue to receive many compliments during the remainder of the year on the attractiveness of our "Christmas tree" as an indoor plant.

Small specimens also make a most unusual centerpiece for a festive table. The Norfolk Island Pine fits the season particularly well because of its symmetrical habit of growth and its attractive green needles. Children will have fun decorating it with tiny ornaments and having their "very own" little Christmas tree.

Our use of the Norfolk Island Pine can be directly attributed to Captain Cook, who discovered Norfolk Island in his second voyage around the world in 1774. It lies some 900 miles (1,448km) east of Australia and about 500 miles (805km) directly north of New Zealand. On this small island, Cook found a magnificent group of evergreens (now known as Norfolk Island Pines) and he made a particular note in his log to the effect that they would make good masts. Though the custom is no longer as popular, these trees were also given as wedding presents by the Dutch.

When Norfolk Island Pines are grown in containers, they will remain comparatively dwarf for a number of years until they reach about 4ft (1.2m) in height and begin to lose their lower branches. Since they tend to be a little top heavy, it's best to grow them in clay containers and I also find that growth will be slower and better if a top soil-based mixture is used rather than an artificial one.

The Norfolk Island Pine is a tiny, perfect Christmas tree.

Use a commercial, tropical plant soil mixture to which you've added one part humus. If you prefer to make up your own mix, use two parts top soil, one part composted cattle manure or material from the home garden compost factory, and one part builder's or horticultural sand. Before planting, place a 1in (2.5cm) layer of pebbles, broken clay pot, or plastic chips in the bottom of the container because good drainage is a must.

Provide a full light location for this plant, but screen it from direct sun between June and September by using sheer drapes. The Norfolk Island Pine likes plenty of fresh air, so open the doors or windows during the frost-free months or move it to a shaded spot outdoors.

From the 1st of March until the beginning of October, water thoroughly twice a week and feed with a soluble, tropical plant food such as an 8-8-8 every two weeks from the first of May until September. Every other year, during March, April, or May, your Norfolk Island Pine will need to be moved to a larger container. Use any of the soil mixtures recommended earlier when repotting.

Palms

An old Islamic tale tells of how, when Allah had created man, he found himself with two lumps of clay left over: one of these he made into a camel, the other he made into a palm tree. The Prophet assured the faithful, "I swear to you, by Him who holds my soul in His hands, that there are palm trees in Paradise."

Be that as it may, this mythical tree was doubtless the Date Palm (*Phoenix dactyfera*) still found growing in great numbers in North Africa and Syria. For the Syrian householder, dwelling in the countryside, a small grove of Date Palms is one of his most valuable assets. It not only provides food for his family, but for his camel and other animals as well.

The indoor gardener with a window of full sun, a fluorescent light set-up or the equivalent, doesn't need to travel to the Middle East or wait for his entrance to Paradise to try his or her hand at growing a Date Palm. A miniature version of those that grow on African oases can be handled easily in an indoor garden and this elegant plant can be grown from the pit of any commercial date.

Make a start by purchasing a package of the best quality dates available. Eat some of them and keep the stones (or seeds, as they should be called.) Since not all of these seeds will germinate, you'll need at least half a dozen. Date seeds take a long time to germinate, so give them a helping hand by gently cracking the outer shell to allow moisture to enter. Uncracked stones can take up to six months to germinate, compared to seven or eight weeks for those that have been cracked.

You'll need three clay or plastic pots measuring 6in (18cm) across the top. Place a 1in (2.5cm) layer of pebbles, broken clay pot, pieces of charcoal, or the new plastic pieces in the bottom of the container to ensure good drainage. Next, fill the pot to the rim with one of the commercial African Violet or tropical plant soil mixtures. Keen indoor gardeners may wish to make up their own mixture out of two parts top soil, one part composted cattle manure or material from the home garden compost factory, and one part builder's or horticultural sand or plastic pieces. Firm the soil mixture down with your fingers and level so the surface is 1/2in (1cm) below the rim of the pot. Give a good soaking with room-temperature water, cover with a plastic bag, and place in a full light location but out of direct sun. During the germination period, you'll probably only need to water once a week.

When the new plants are 2 to 3in (5-6.5cm) high, move them to a full sun location, or place them under an artificial light set-up. Soak them thoroughly twice a week until the first of October and then drop back to once a week. From April until the beginning of September, feed every two weeks with one of the soluable, complete, tropical plant foods such as an 8-8-8.

Your Date Palm will need to be moved to a larger container in March or April each year until it is 2ft (.6m) tall. Again, use the soil mixture as recommended for germinating seeds. From then on, your Date Palm will only need repotting in a larger container every three or four years. Under good growing conditions, it will reach up to 6ft (1.8m) at maturity.

Other palms which are suitable for growing indoors and require the same treatment as the Date Palm, are: Chamaedora, Howea, and Syagrus. The Dwarf Palm (*Neanthe elegans*) will grow well, given high humidity and plenty of indirect light. This palm should be watered freely in the summer and fed regularly throughout the growing season. During the winter, water sparingly, don't feed, and only repot when the Dwarf Palm is pot-bound.

Philodendrons

There are probably more Philodendrons sold by commercial plant growers than any other indoor plant. They are the easiest of all foliage plants to grow, given indirect light, a soil barely moist at all times, and normal indoor temperatures of 68 to 72°F (20-22°C).

Philodendrons have the ability to tolerate low light conditions as well or better than many of the tropical foliage plants, but this does not mean that they won't grow better under high light conditions. From the beginning of November to the 1st of March, when the sun's rays are slanted and not very strong, a sunny window is an excellent location for them.

I like to work a rotation system with Philodendrons. Every week or ten days I move the plants in the darker part of the room to a well-lit window and replace them with others. This will ensure healthier and much better looking plants. Philodendrons also grow particularly well under fluorescent lights.

The commercial plant grower will have Philodendrons growing in a rich soil, so it's best not to feed them for the first four months after you take them home. After that, they should be fed every four months during the eight month, high light season. During the dark months, one feeding with the same soluble, complete, tropical plant food will be all that's required.

Keep the leaves attractive and clean by misting them under the shower with room-temperature water once a week. A daily syringing of the leaves will also keep them attractive and remove the dust that may have settled on them.

The heart-leaved Philodendron, taken from Jamaica to England by Captain Bligh, is one of our most popular trailing or climbing vines; in nature it trails, but it will climb equally well if given adequate support. Many people use a piece of driftwood or some bark-covered lumber to provide the needed support.

In the early stages of growth, the leaves of the Philodendron are about 3in (7.5cm) long. However, if planted in a rich soil in a hobby greenhouse or conservatory, they'll often reach 15in (38cm) in length.

The lush green leaves of a Philodendron cascade down behind a screen of graceful palm fronds.

Heart-leaved Philodendrons are one of the very few plants that will grow equally well in soil or water. When grown in water, warm water must be constantly added as it is used up or evaporated. Small pieces of barbecue charcoal in the bottom of the container will keep the water sweet. Every three weeks add 1T (15ml) of soluble, complete, tropical plant food, following the manufacturer's directions.

Philodendrons grown in soil or artificial mixtures are best set on a plastic or metal humidity tray filled to within 1/2in (1cm) of the top with pebbles, gravel, or some of the new plastic pieces used for this purpose. Water is added and maintained so that its level is just below the bottom of the containers.

During the four month dark period beginning in November, keep the soil barely moist by watering no more than once a week. For the other eight months, water every five days, just enough to keep the growing medium moist.

Most Philodendrons will need repotting every second year. This can really be done at anytime, but you can expect the best results in March or April when the days have begun to lengthen and brighten considerably. Use a commercial, tropical plant mixture and add one part humus, or make up your own from equal parts top soil, humus, and coarse horticultural or builder's sand. (You can substitute the new ground-up plastic pieces for sand.) Newly potted plants won't need any feeding for four months.

You can propagate your Philodendrons by taking cuttings from the ends of stems and rooting them in perlite or a mixture of sand and peat moss. Also, many mail order seed catalogues carry seeds for Philodendrons and other indoor plants. The best time to start your plants from seed is during the three month period beginning in February. After sowing, you'll need to maintain the temperature of the medium at 75 to 80°F (24-27°C) which means the containers will probably need some bottom heat. The first seedlings should appear in 15 to 30 days.

There are approximately 400 members of the Philodendron family, all of which will do well as indoor plants when given this kind of simple treatment.

Ponytail Palm

The Ponytail Palm, or Elephant's Foot Tree (*Beaucarnea recurvata*), is a hardy succulent belonging to the same family as the Century Plant. It is virtually indestructible, able to go a month without watering. Out in the Mexican desert where it's found growing wild, it can store a year's supply of water in its large, swollen base which resembles a huge bulb covered with elephant's hide. In nature, this caudex, as it's correctly called, becomes several feet (.9-1.2m) across and the branchless trunk reaches 20ft (6m) or more in height. The trunk is topped with a dense and beautiful fountain of leaves which cascade down to the ground.

Healthy indoor specimens which are taken outdoors in the summer will sometimes produce small, white, mildly fragrant blossoms in loosely branched clusters.

The Ponytail should receive at least four hours of sunshine daily, but will also grow well under fluorescent lights which provide moderately high light for 12 hours a day. An ideal location for this plant would be in a north window where there's plenty of bright, indirect light.

While it's normally a slow growing plant, you can speed things up by increased watering and feeding as long as you don't overdo it. This means giving the Ponytail a good soaking and then letting the earth dry out before adding more water. Feed with a complete, tropical plant food, such as an 8-8-8, once in the spring and again in the fall. When the plant has reached the desired size, a much slower rate of growth can be maintained by watering only when the earth is powder-dry and limiting feeding to once each spring.

The Ponytail Palm will not need repotting more frequently than every five years. When it's time to repot, use one of the commercial, tropical soil mixtures or make up your own out of equal parts top soil, humus, and builder's or horticultural sand.

You can easily create new plants by potting up the offshoots which appear on the sides of the base each spring. Alternatively, you can start the Ponytail from seed, sown anytime of year. Started plants are generally available from the better garden stores, nurseries, and garden centers as well.

Pothos

The Pothos [*Scindapsus*] is a climbing or trailing vine, variously known as Devil's Ivy, Golden Pothos, Hunter's Robe, or Solomon Islands Ivy. It's a member of the Arum family and is one of the most successful and easy-to-grow plants under low light conditions.

Most of the Pothos are native to the Solomon Islands, Borneo, and other parts of the South Pacific. There are two kinds which are widely sold: one has green and creamy-yellow foliage; the other has lovely dark green leaves, spotted with creamy-white. Both can be grown with great success under low light conditions.

To grow the Pothos indoors, pieces of cedar with the bark still attached or one of the new porous, light-weight plastic stakes will provide the right kind of support if you wish to treat it as a climbing vine. Alternatively, you can place the Pothos on a mantel or shelf, or in a basket, and let it trail down.

I find the Pothos to be one of the very few plants that will do quite well in the light provided by an incandescent lamp. Under such conditions, the leaves lose quite a bit of their golden color and revert to an almost solid green, but they still remain very attractive. When grown where there's plenty of natural light or under fluorescent lighting, the true colors will develop and the vines will grow vigorously. An ideal plant for locating in a north window, the Pothos will also flourish when set 3 to 5ft (.9-1.5m) in from windows facing in other directions. During the dark months of November, December, January, and February, it can safely be grown on the sill of any window.

Coming as it does from the steaming jungles of the Solomon Islands and Borneo means that plenty of moisture will be required in the surrounding air. To provide ideal growing conditions, you'll need to use some form of mechanical humidification and it will also help to set the plants in a tray, two-thirds full of pebbles or gravel. Keep the tray filled with water at all times so that it's within 1/2in (1cm) of the bottoms of the containers. Have a plant syringe handy and mist both sides of the leaves at least once a day, using warm water. Because of the high humidity, the bathroom makes an ideal plant hospital and, provided there's a window or some form of artificial light, the Pothos and many other plants will thrive there and add a decorative touch.

In the light months, the plants will need watering every three or

A font of spiked fronds and a bulbous base make the Ponytail an unusual palm.

Variegated leaves add character to the Pothos.

four days. During the four months starting with November, when the light intensity is low, allow the surface of the soil mixture to start feeling dry before you water again. Feed the Pothos with a complete, soluble, tropical plant food, such as an 8-8-8, every two weeks when you water, except during the winter when no feeding at all will be required.

The Pothos likes to be potbound, so repot no more often than every second year and preferably every third. Use one of the commercial, tropical plant soils and add one part humus. If you wish to make up your own potting mixture, use equal parts of top soil, humus, and coarse horticultural or builder's sand.

Because it grows so fast, the Pothos will probably need to be vigorously pruned back to a 6in (15cm) stub every third year. During the summer, new plants are easily propagated by rooting the tips of healthy stems in water or in a mixture of sand and peat moss.

Rex Begonias

Another of the favorite indoor plants of Victorian and Edwardian homes was the Rex or Foliage Begonia. It went out of favor in North America with the introduction of the African Violet in the late 1920's and the depression days of the 1930's. It stayed that way until about 20 years ago when new hybrids were developed whose leaves offer a fascinating range of colors and patterns. The plants also produce blooms but these are insignificant when compared with the beautifully colored and textured leaves which rival costly fabrics.

The Begonia family is one of the major ones of the plant world with over 2,500 known members. One variety was found growing on the Caribbean island of Santa Dominga by the French botanist, Charles Plumier and he named the new plant in honor of Michel Begon, the Island's governor, who had aided in his search for plants.

Rex Begonias were accidentally introduced to the western world in a sheaf of orchids, sent from Assam in India by J. Simon. By 1858 the new Begonia was being sold commercially. Thousands of hybrids were then developed and the Rex Begonia was on its way to world-wide fame.

Rex Begonias are very happy indoors, given proper care. In general, these plants will be healthier and their leaves more colorful if they are kept out of direct sunlight. This rule does not apply to plants that receive only half a day in full sun, nor does it apply during the dark months of winter when Begonias can be located in any window. In the light months, a good place for Rex Begonias is in a north-facing window, or in about 3ft (.9m) from one facing west or east. The ideal location, however, is under fluorescent lights; such artificial lighting will intensify the colors and patterns of the foliage.

Rex Begonias are completely at home in the 70 to 72°F (21-22°C) temperatures found indoors, though lowering the heat to 65°F (18°C) at night is advisable. Be careful of sudden changes in temperature, though, which can be harmful to all plants. It can be very damaging to expose your plants to a cold blast of air from an open door or window, or a sudden rush of hot air from a radiator or a forced air register.

In order to enjoy real success with Rex Begonias, you must ensure that the air surrounding them contains plenty of moisture; these plants require higher humidity than any other member of the Begonia family.

As I have mentioned many times in this book, without some form of mechanical humidification the air found in homes and offices is usually dryer than the Sahara Desert. Very few plants will thrive under such conditions and this is particularly true of the Rex Begonia.

Most indoor plants need only 35 per cent humidity. Varieties with heavy textured leaves will do well where the humidity is between 40 and 50 per cent, and those with delicate leaves may need 50 to 60 per cent. For Rex Begonias, the humidity reading should be about 50 per cent. You can use any type of mechanical humidifier to achieve this level and you can also increase the moisture in the air by setting your plants on a 2in (5cm) layer of pebbles in a metal or plastic tray. This is kept partially filled with water which will gradually evaporate into the air surrounding the plants. Make sure that the bottoms of the containers don't come in direct contact with the water or moisture will be drawn up by the roots, causing them to rot. Rex Begonias are particularly susceptible to this condition because of their root system.

The roots of almost all Rex Begonias tend to rot easily when overwatered. This is because the main roots are actually horizontally extended stems, or rhizomes, often enlarged by food storage. It's important, then, to use the correct pots. Plastic containers are inexpensive and universally used for most indoor plants but are not satisfactory for the Rex Begonia. The best containers are either clay pots or wire baskets lined with moss. The porous clay will allow the air to pass freely through the soil mixture, as will the moss-lined wire basket, providing good insurance against too much moisture.

For the same reason, proper drainage and careful watering are vitally important with Rex Begonias. Place two or three pieces of broken clay pot over the drainage hole of your container and add a 1in (2.5cm) layer of broken charcoal pieces whenever you repot. These plants should be watered only when the surface of the soil is beginning to dry out, using room-temperature water.

Regular feeding is a must; only when Rex Begonias are correctly fed will the colorful leaves be at their best. I like to use a soluble, complete tropical plant food, such as an 8-8-8, every two weeks during the active period of growth. As you become more experienced, you may wish to add a little blood meal to the soil, to intensify the color of the leaves. Blood meal is available from garden stores, nurseries, and garden centers.

Bacteria in the soil mixture surrounding your plants is essential to their production of food. Because the bacterial count in the soil usually drops dramatically after two years, it pays to repot the majority of indoor plants every second year. Again, the Rex Begonia is an exception to the rule and should only be repotted when the root system completely fills the container, when it is potbound. I find that Begonias treated in this manner are more compact and uniform.

The soil mixture for Rex Begonias must be rich in humus. One of the commercial, tropical plant mixtures can be used, but you must make this one-quarter peat moss and one-quarter leaf mold. The indoor gardener who prefers to create his own mixture should use the formula of four parts top soil: four parts peat moss: three parts leaf mold: two parts coarse builder's or horticultural sand.

There will be a period during the year when the plants go partially dormant, with very slow growth; or completely dormant, with the loss of all their leaves. Don't feed or repot the plants until they resume active growth.

Since Rex Begonias will tend to become tall and long-stemmed, they will eventually need to be replaced with new plants, either purchased or started from your own cuttings.

Cuttings can be made in two ways. One method is to choose a healthy, fairly mature leaf with about 1in (2.5cm) of stalk attached. Turn it upside down on a hard surface such as a kitchen cutting board and cut through its main veins in a number of places with a sharp knife. Next, prepare a plastic seedling flat by filling it two-thirds full with equal parts peat and coarse horticultural or builder's sand. Thoroughly dampen the mixture with warm water and then make a hole to receive the stalk of the begonia cutting. Make sure the leaf is lying flat and right-side-up on the surface of the rooting medium and cover the seeding flat with a piece of glass or plastic. During the rooting period keep the tray in the same full light location as you would choose for mature plants, the best possible place being under a fluorescent light set-up. It won't be long until little plantlets start to grow where you have made cuts in the leaves. Once these are 1in (2.5cm) high, pot them up in 3in (7.5cm) clay containers using the same soil mixture as recommended previously for repotting Rex Begonias. When the containers are filled with roots of 2 to 3in (5-7.5cm) in length, the plants can be moved to larger clay or moss-lined containers.

An alternative method of rooting a new plant is to select a healthy leaf with a 1-1/2in (3.5cm) stalk. Place the leaf, stem down, in a glass of water that is small enough to support it, or cover the glass with a piece of plastic wrap, poke a hole through it, and insert the stalk. Add a small piece of charcoal to keep the water sweet. In about three weeks roots will form on the stalk and new growth will appear at the leaf joint. As soon as the roots are about 1in (2.5cm) in length, pot up the leaf in a 3in (7.5cm) container using the usual soil mixture. Just as soon as new growth is developing vigorously, you can cut away the mother leaf.

Rex Begonias rival costly fabrics in richness of color and texture.

Strawberry Begonias

As mentioned before, one of the major problems facing any indoor gardener is poor light conditions. An excellent way to avoid this situation is to choose plants that have a proven record of success where the light is quite low. Just such a plant is the Strawberry Begonia (*Saxifraga sarmentosa*). Other common names include Pedlar's Basket and Mother of Thousands; the latter refers to the plantlets produced on the tips of the runners which root extremely easily. The name Strawberry Begonia can be confusing because it is neither a member of the strawberry nor of the Begonia family. The reference to strawberries comes from the fact that the plants throw out runners in much the same way as the fruit.

Strawberry Begonias are grown mainly as foliage plants whose dark green leaves have white veins on top and red underneath, creating a delightful contrast. I particularly like the variegated form, whose colorful green foliage is edged with creamy white. In May and early summer, clusters of rather insignificant, crimson-spotted, white blossoms appear on the plants.

While a full light location is preferable for the Strawberry Begonia, it should be shaded from direct sunlight from May through September by using a sheer drape to filter out the strong rays of the sun. I don't know of a better plant to use under growth lamps, particularly under a table lamp with one of the comparatively new screw-in plant bulbs.

This indoor foliage plant is not happy if the temperature rises above 70 °F (21 °C) in the daytime. It should be dropped back to at least 60 °F (16 °C) during the evening hours for that all-important rest period required by all indoor plants.

Feed every two weeks from the 1st of April until the beginning of October with one of the soluble, complete, tropical plant foods such as an 8-8-8.

Allow the surface of the potting mixture to become dry between thorough soakings with room-temperature water. A daily syringing of the leaves, also with warm water, helps to supply the humid atmosphere they require. It also pays to set the plant on a small tray filled with pebbles or the new pieces of horticultural plastic. Add sufficient water so that its level is maintained just below the bottom of the container at all times.

The Strawberry Begonia should be grown in a shallow clay or plastic pot or pottery bowl using a humusy tropical plant mixture. Take one of the commercial mixtures and add an extra part leafmold, material from the home garden compost factory, composted cattle manure, or peat moss. Normally, the earth is pressed quite firmly around the roots of any indoor plant but the Strawberry Begonia is the exception to the rule. It likes the soil to be very loose around its roots. Repotting is best done in March or April.

There are two excellent ways of rooting the little plantlets that develop on the tips of the runners. One is to place a small 3in (7.5cm) clay or plastic pot filled with a tropical plant soil mixture beside the mother plant and place the tip in the earth. When the roots have formed (in about three weeks) the new plant is cut from the runner that attached it to the mother plant. The other method is to take a plastic seedling tray and fill it with tropical plant soil to within 1/2in (1cm) of the top. Place the mother plant in the center with the runners radiating out from it like the spokes of a wheel and set the little plantlet at the tip of each runner in the earth. In about three weeks, roots will have formed and you'll have a number of plants ready to be detached from the mother plant and potted up in 3in (7.5cm) clay or plastic containers.

Scheffleras

One of the most striking of the large indoor plants, with its exotic foliage and bold dimensions, is the Schefflera. This native of Australia is happiest in partial shade but, surprisingly, it is tough enough to withstand both full sun and quite poor lighting. The Schefflera will also do particularly well when grown under fluorescent lights.

Scheffleras relish a sponging of their leaves every week to ten days and a daily misting will help keep the surrounding air humid and get rid of dust that can clog the pores of the foliage. Another way to eliminate accumulated dust is to put your plants under the shower, using warm water, every week or ten days.

Much healthier growth will be produced if you allow the soil surrounding the roots to become quite dry before giving the plant a thorough soaking with lukewarm water. Avoid overfeeding the Schefflera as well - two feedings a year, one at the beginning of March and another at the beginning of September, will be sufficient. Use a soluble, complete tropical plant food such as an 8-8-8.

When repotting becomes necessary, it's best to do it in March or April. Buy one of the tropical plant soil mixtures and add one part humus, or make up your own using equal parts top soil, humus, and coarse horticultural or builder's sand.

The exotic foliage of the Schefflera is as striking as its bold dimensions.

The Spider Plant [opposite page] is a fountain of gently arching leaves and delicate runners.

Spider Plants

The Spider Plant [*Chlorophytum*] was discovered in the 1800's in South Africa and became very widely grown in England in Victorian and Edwardian times. The popular Spider Plant is grown for its arching, grass-like leaves which are colored either green and white or green and

yellow. In the spring and summer the plants throw out long, wiry runners with little plantlets on the ends. This gives them a spidery appearance and, hence, the name.

To maintain its attractive appearance, the Spider Plant needs a location where it will receive as much indirect light as possible. It will grow well in a north window year-round, but if it's in a south window from May to October, there should be a sheer drape between the plant and the hot summer sun. Plants growing in windows which face east or west will need the same protection. The Spider Plant is also ideal for growing under fluorescent lights.

These plants will need a good soaking with warm water twice a week during the growing season and in the winter should be watered every five or six days. Browning of the tips of the leaves can be a sign of overwatering, but it's more likely caused by watering with chlorinated or fluoridated tap water. Either let the water stand overnight, or use one of the bottled waters which are widely available.

From the 1st of March until November, feed the plants once a month with a soluble, tropical plant food such as a 8-8-8. No feeding will be required during the dark months that follow.

The level of humidity doesn't need to be too high for this plant — your hygrometer should read from 20 to 30 per cent. Nevertheless plants not growing in hanging baskets will benefit from being placed in a tray filled with 2in (5cm) of gravel or pebbles and sufficient water to bring the level up to within 1/2in (1cm) of the bottom of the container.

Sooner or later, the Spider Plants will grow to such a size that their thick, white, fleshy roots will fill the pot and start to show above the surface of the soil. When this occurs, it's time to either move the entire plant to a larger container or divide it and form several new ones. March or April is the best time to do this. Shake off the excess soil from the roots and repot using a commercial, tropical plant mixture to which you've added one part humus. You can also make up your own mixture with equal parts of top soil, humus, and coarse horticultural or builder's sand. It's very important to place a 1in (2.5cm) layer of pebbles, broken clay pot, or pieces of charcoal in the bottom of the container for drainage purposes.

The little plantlets on the ends of the runners can also be set in soil in a container close by the mother plant and when rooted can be cut from the runner. They will root easily in water as well, just follow the same procedure.

A word of warning. You'll find that the tapering leaves of the Spider Plant are quite sensitive. They resent being touched by humans or animals, so keep them out of reach.

Succulents

The various members of the succulent family make almost foolproof indoor plants and also grow well in containers or in the garden. Succulents are rosette-forming plants which, over thousands of years, have developed thick, fleshy leaves that can store sizeable amounts of water against periods of drought. This means that they're able to grow and thrive with much less moisture than other plants. Although most succulents are quite tender, they do so well under the warm, dry conditions found in modern homes and offices that, in the autumn, you can take plants growing outdoors inside for the winter without doing them any harm. They are easily propagated by taking the offsets, or suckers, which form at the base of the plants and potting them up in the fall.

Bloom is not always important with succulents as their fleshy leaves are often brilliantly colored. In the past, succulents were very popular for planting in ribbons or designs because of their neat habit of growth. This type of gardening reached its height during the Victorian era, the most spectacular example being Lyndhurst, the former home of Jay Gould which was located on the Hudson River in New York State. A series of greenhouses, each 250ft (76m) long, produced enough succulents to plant masses of gardens in elaborate patterns. The art of gardening in this fashion is experiencing a rivival after many dormant years, since the severe lines and undecorated walls of modern dwellings provide the perfect foil for these decorative plantings.

The *Aloe vera*, a remarkable succulent, has been grown for medicinal and decorative purposes for well over 3,000 years. Originating in Egypt and other countries of the Middle East, the *Aloe vera* has been named the "true Aloe" because it exhibits the best medicinal qualities of all these plants. It's a semi-tropical and tropical plant so I'm able to grow it with great success in my garden in Bermuda. I've proven the value of its medicinal properties many times: it soothes and heals minor cuts, scalds, and burns; a small piece of the stem makes a soothing substitute styptic pencil for treating shaving accidents; and it relieves the effects of insect bites and poison ivy when the Aloe gel is prepared in a poultice. (Aloe gel is now being added to shampoos and hair conditioners and is available commercially.)

I don't know of another indoor plant that is much easier to grow,

and it's almost completely pest-free. The *Aloe vera,* or Bitter Aloe as it is also called, will develop leaves measuring 1 to 2ft (.3-.6cm) in length and grows in the typical rosette form of the succulents. Give it a full sun location if at all possible; it prefers a minimum of four hours of sunshine each day. I've grown it successfully in windows facing south, east, and west and it will need 12 hours of light a day when grown under fluorescent or other growth lamps.

Succulents are easy to overwater. Allow the surface of the soil to become moderately dry between waterings — try a good soaking once a week in the beginning. Very little fertilizer will be required and an established plant should be fed once in March and again in October, using one of the soluble, complete, tropical plant foods such as an 8-8-8. Newly potted plants should not be fed.

An ideal soil mixture for any of the succulents would be a half-and-half mixture of one of the tropical plant soil mixtures and builder's or horticultural sand or plastic pieces. To each gallon (4.5L) of this mixture, add a tablespoon (15ml) of ground horticultural limestone and bone meal.

South Africa has given our indoor gardens the Partridge Breast Aloe, or *Aloe variegata,* another slow-growing, perennial succulent. The leaves are triangular in shape and colored a rich, dark green, attractively marked and margined in white. I like the pink to red colored blooms which are showy, tubular in shape, average 1-1/2in (3.5cm) in length and are carried in loose clusters on stalks growing 12in (30cm) long. Flowering time is from late spring to mid-summer. Give the Partridge Breast Aloe exactly the same growing conditions as you would for the Bitter Aloe.

All Aloes are splendid succulents, and the Aloe vera [right] in particular is widely used for its remarkable medicinal qualities.

Index

African Violet, 21, 22, 23-25
Air, 17
Air-layering, 20, 61
Aloes, 93-94
Aphids, 21-22
Aspidistra, 26-27

Bacteria, 85
Begonias, 84-87

Cacti, 28-30 *See also* Flowering Cacti
Caladium, 31-33
Calamondin Orange, 41-43
Cape Primrose, 34-35
Carnivorous Plants, 36-37
Chinese Evergreen, 38-39
Cissus, 40, 43
Citrus Trees, 41-43
Cleaning of plants, 15, 16
Cobra Lily, 36
Coleus, 18, 44-45
Cordylines, 46-47
Croton, 48-49, 51
Crown Cactus, 30
Cuttings, 19

Dieffenbachia, 20, 50, 51
Diseases, 21, 22
Dracaena, 20, 51, 52
Drainage, 13, 15
Dust, 15-16

Elephant's Foot Tree, 81, 83

Feeding, 15
Ferns, 55-57
Ficus, 58-62
Fiddle Leaf Fig, 61-62
Flowering Cacti, 53-54
Foliage Begonia, 84-87

Gardenia, 63-64
Gloxinia, 65-67

Hawaiian Ti Plant, 46-47
Hooded Trumpet, 36
Hospital for plants, 18, 82
Hoya, 68-70
Humidity, 11-12
Huntsman's Horn, 36
Hygrometer, 32, 56, 91

Impatiens, 71
India Rubber Plant, 61-62

Kangaroo Ivy, 40, 43

Leaves, 10, 13, 15-16
Light, 8, 9, 10

Mealy bugs, 22, 29

Narcissus, 72-73
New Zealand Grass Palm, 46-47
Norfolk Island Pine, 74-75

Owl's Eye, 29

Palms, 76-78
Pests, 21-22
Philodendrons, 19, 20, 78-80
Photosynthesis, 10
Pin Cushion, 30
Pitcher Plant, 36, 37
Plant bombs, 21, 22
Ponytail Palm, 81, 83
Pothos, 82-83
Pots, 13, 15
Prickly Pear, 30

Rattail Cactus, 30
Rex Begonia, 84-87
Roots, 12, 13, 15
Runners, 88, 89, 91, 92

Scale insects, 22
Schefflera, 90
Seeds, 18
Soil mixtures, 17
Spider mites, 21, 22
Spider Plant, 91-92
Spraying, 21, 22
Sterilizing Soil, 22
Strawberry Begonia, 88-89
Succulents, 93-94
Sundew, 36, 37
Sweet Trumpet, 36

Temperature, 10-11
Trays, 12

Venus Fly Trap, 37

Watering, 12-15
Wax Plant, 68-70
Weeping Fig, 60-62
White flies, 21
Winter, as dormancy period, 10, 12, 13, 15, 29, 60, 64, 67, 80

NOTE: Such topics as Diseases, Feeding, Humidity, Light, Propagation, Soil Mixtures, Temperature, and Watering are also discussed in the sections on individual plants.